Praise for *Recover Your Good Heart*

I cannot recommend Jim Robbins' book *Recover Your Good Heart* highly enough. With profound insight, compassion, and solid biblical support, he resurrects one of the most forgotten and overlooked truths in our day—We are not the same people coming out of conversion that we were going in! Our sin nature and old heart are not eradicated but they are offset with a glorious, unalterable, supernatural reality. We have new hearts, new inclinations, and a new identity. We are far more than forgiven sinners. We are renovated saints with new hearts, good hearts; which come wholly through the Holy Spirit. Thank you Jim for reminding us that our hope for godliness is not gritting our teeth and trying harder. It is falling back on the resources and power of our good heart, the "heart of flesh", birthed at conversion and appropriated throughout our lifetime. A great work!

> **Dwight Edwards, author of *Revolution Within***
> and advisor to Larry Crabb
> www.kindlingforthefire.com

"I live in the UK and would love to get further copies here to give to friends and others. I loved the book! ... It's refreshingly true, telling me that I'm actually 'more than ok', and the way the Father truly sees and relates to me. It builds up self-esteem by renewing the mind with what is actually fact, not just platitudes. I underlined most of it, and have lent it to a friend who I warned about the underlining... I've gone back over and over to my underlinings, and to contemplate the context of the underlinings, and every time it seems that the truth penetrates even deeper - truly Scriptural, as my life changes a little more each time. How can I find the words to affirm you for the words you've put to paper?

I am also a Biblical counsellor and train other counsellors, so the book will become one of my 'I urge you to read this' books. It really is a 'must read if you want to change' book."

> Jenny L.
> *Harpenden, United Kingdom*

"'Amazing Grace how sweet the sound that saved a wretch like me.' In my practice as a Christian Counselor, I often hear that my clients still think of themselves as a wretch; shameful and dirty. They tell me that they are "sinners saved by grace" and that their "heart is deceitful above all things." But that is who they were, not who they are now.

Christians today live in bondage because they still think of themselves as they were before salvation and don't understand their new identity in Christ. Jim Robbins has written a much needed book that in great Biblical detail and with tender and powerful truth helps the reader to embrace the fact that God has given them a new heart to replace the old, deceitful one and a new identity as holy and forgiven rather than sinner. *Recover Your Good Heart* is a healing, freeing, and empowering must read for every Christ follower."

Kim West, M.Div.
Phoenix, Arizona
www.make-my-Christian-life-work.com
www.solutions-Christian-counseling.com

"Ah, yes … thanks for referencing my recommendation of *Recover Your Good Heart*. Yes! I suggest it for everyone! Growing up in the modern church, I was taught (repeatedly) that my heart was so foul, evil and awful. Thus, if one is told that, one eventually believes that and thus, *lives* like that. It was when I read this book, that the Holy Spirit so beautifully showed me that upon salvation, Papa gave me *his* heart which is *totally* and completely good. After all, God is only love. And God gives only that which is *good*. And because upon salvation I received a totally new heart, it was a heart filled with the Spirit of Jesus Christ. Thus, *knowing* this and *believing* this absolute truth, I realized, was so incredibly important for me to realize *who* I am and that I have a good heart. Once I *got* this, it completely blew my mind—for the good."

Amy C.
Surprise, Arizona
http://amyiswalkinginthespirit.blogspot.com/

"'Restoration,' 'recovery,' 'revival' are buzzwords in church circles these days but most of what is being preached from pulpits is just recycled versions of the phrase "God is good, you are bad, try harder". Jim Robbins adds his thoughts to the growing number of believers who are finding out that our life in Jesus is not about more effort and busyness but about the discovery that we are loved by our Father who is ready to share His life with us without restraint. It reminds me of the scene from the *Lion, the Witch, and the Wardrobe* in which the stone statues in the courtyard of the witch's castle are breathed upon by Aslan and brought back to life. This book is life-giving."

Fran M.
Portland, Oregon

"If you have ever been to church and left feeling empty, condemned, tired, or not good enough; this is an essential read. As Christians we sometimes forget God's promises of forgiveness and feel as though we have to do things to earn God's love. Well, we don't! Neither do we have to work to "be better". God gave us a good heart. This book is an up-lifting read that uses scripture and Biblical truth to show us the goodness of our hearts accomplished by God's work and that we are fully approved and accepted by him. *Recover Your Good Heart* will reveal Biblical truths to you and encourage you to live from your heart. I cannot recommend it more."

Meredith M.
Tampa, Florida

A few months ago I was having a conversation with a very close family member. He responded to something I said with, "The heart is desperately wicked." That comment never sat well with me, but I didn't know why. [*Recover Your Good Heart*] has put words to that discomfort and has taught me where it came from— from a new, good heart placed in me by a loving, good God so He and I can relate in a new way. As a result, I am free, and you can be too! Thank you, Jim Robbins!

Chris P.
Woodland Park, Colorado
http://1freebeliever.blogspot.com/

JIM ROBBINS

RECOVER YOUR GOOD HEART—

Living free from religious guilt and the shame of not good–enough

RECOVER YOUR GOOD HEART

Published by Kindle Ink Press, 2008.

Cover photo: Jeffrey Van Daele, LOSTBEAR Photography.
           Courtesy, Big Stock Photo.com.

ISBN-13: 978-0-615-24853-0

TABLE OF CONTENTS

Acknowledgements

- To Dwight Edwards, for his encouragement, kindness and support. I am deeply grateful.

- Larry Crabb, Dwight Edwards, and John Eldredge and *Ransomed Heart*, for removing the veil of religion from my eyes and giving me back the Gospel.

- John, Meredith, Cindy, Dennis and James for their gracious willingness to share their stories.

- Dwight Edwards, Meredith Martin, Jenny Lowen, Kim West, Amy Chiaramonte, Chris Pack, and Fran Means for the thoughtful reviews.

- David, Loren and Bob at *Family Room Media*. — www.familyroommedia.com

- To blogger, Aida Calder, for her expert P.R. skills! — www.forgettingtheformerthings.blogspot.com

- Andy Havens of *Sanestorm Marketing* for the great blog. — www.sanestorm.com

- Dallas Willard, for helping me to see the Kingdom more clearly.

- My wife, Lynn, for her tireless editing skills and sacrifices. I couldn't be a writer without you. You are my "Arwen."

- Olivia and Nate, my children, who always bring life to me.

Introduction

When generations of Christians have been given a truncated view of the very message they've set their hopes upon, it is difficult and often impossible to breach that entrenched view. This book is an attempt to restore what has been lost to recent generations of Christians. Some readers will discover what they suspected was true all along, yet wonder why they've never heard this message. Some will reject the message simply because it does not line up with their long-held assumptions. Mark Twain once said that, "Often, the surest way to convey misinformation is to tell the strict truth."

It's possible to be forgiven, and yet not free. It takes something in addition to the grace of forgiveness to free people from what hinders them. You may be forgiven, yet bound; pardoned, yet encumbered. — And the heart is at the center of all that. Generations of Christians have been pinned down by some very disabling assumptions about their hearts that have left them both unhealed and untransformed. This book questions those assumptions in light of Scripture, and offers the rest of the Gospel most of us have never been told. The message of this book is not a new teaching. Rather, it is the recovery of what has been known through ages past, yet lost to the recent generations of Christians.

The book you hold is for those who have suspected that something was missing in the message they have been hearing, and who want to live more fully in the Kingdom as they discover the surprising truth about their hearts.

"To be believed, make the truth unbelievable."

– Napoleon Bonaparte

Is that actually true?

The answers to the following questions may surprise you. Note: You may find yourself answering the questions differently once you proceed through the book!

---

1. **True or False?** The Christian's heart is just as sinful after becoming a Christian as it was before becoming one.

2. **True or False?** The Christian's heart is a mixture of good and bad.

3. **True or False?** A Christian's heart is totally good and pure.

4. **True or False?** Christianity is about right behavior and morality.

6. **True or False?** God is interested in fixing us.

7. **True or False?** Jesus' primary offer to us is the forgiveness of sins.

CHAPTER ONE

What have you been told about your heart?

(The 'gospel' of guilt, shame, and pressure)

"The revolution of Jesus is in the first place and continuously a
revolution of the human heart or spirit."
– Dallas Willard, *Renovation of the Heart*[1]

A t certain points in the book, you will see questions that I posed to
Christians I know. I was attempting to get at the message they were
being told about their heart—even after becoming Christians. These friends
come from different church backgrounds and experiences, yet their stories
are indicative of some sad realities facing Christians today. I suspect their
stories are more common than you may think.

Question: "There's a hymn that says we are 'prone to wander'—meaning
that it's our nature and tendency, even as Christians, to stray from God. Do
you believe that to be true?"

Meredith, from Tampa: "Christians are so often told that we are unworthy
sinners and not worthy to be in His presence, that we avoid him in an attempt
to hide ourselves from Him."

Right diagnosis, wrong treatment

Medical mistakes can be made by the most capable and trained doctors. A patient's condition can be misdiagnosed or mistreated, with dire results. Doctor Jerome Groopman, author of the revealing book *How Doctors Think*, tells us from his own medical experience what can happen—for he too had failed to correctly diagnose and treat a patient—with painful consequences:

> One of my patients was a middle-aged woman with seemingly endless complaints whose voice sounded to me like a nail scratching a blackboard. One day she had a new complaint, discomfort in her upper chest. I tried to pin down what caused the discomfort—eating, exercising, coughing—to no avail. Then I ordered routine tests, including a chest X-ray and a cardiogram. Both were normal. In desperation, I prescribed antacids. But her complaint persisted, and I became deaf to it. In essence, I couldn't think in a different way. Several weeks later, I was stat-paged to the emergency room. My patient had a dissecting aortic aneurysm, a life-threatening tear of the large artery that carries blood from the heart to the rest of the body. She died. ... I have never forgiven myself for failing to diagnose it.[2]

Either misdiagnosing an illness or mistreating it can prove disastrous. What happens when your quality of life depends upon the correct judgment of a professional whom you believe to be trained and capable, yet you discover he has given you the wrong "cure"? Or perhaps you are seeing a therapist for treatment of depression. You and your past are thoroughly analyzed and you're given some emotional goals to work through; yet the real problem is somewhere deeper, at a level that analysis won't touch—and you remain stuck.

In any of these cases, you are told that the prescribed treatment will work, yet you are not getting better; perhaps worse in some ways. A problem, rightly discerned, but wrongly treated can only lead to further sickness.

The Church in our days has responded with the wrong course of treatment for our greatest needs. What we call the "Gospel" today (which *is* the solution to humanity's condition) is at best a weakened and impoverished gospel, and at worst, not the Gospel at all. We have provided the wrong cure. We have incorrectly treated the disease—with disturbing results: our churches are full of people who remain enfeebled with shame, guilt, and futility. They are pinned down by the same things they struggled with before becoming Christians and are anything *but* restored, free citizens of the Kingdom. In fact, many leaders *use* shame in order to get their congregants to "be more committed, serve more, do more."

Many have felt cheated by the Christian "cure" they have been given. Not intentionally deceived, to be sure. There were no preachers or Sunday School teachers who set out to mislead them, for those good-hearted leaders have passed on simply what *they've* been given. What most of us who call ourselves 'Christians' have been told about the Gospel is, at best, partially true: We have been told that Christianity is about getting your sins forgiven and going to heaven. This is true, yet grossly incomplete. The deceptive story line running throughout our modern Christian story is that you are merely forgiven, yet unchanged: that you've been pardoned and are going to heaven, but you remain essentially the same person you've always been. We've been left as Lazarus, called out of the tomb, yet still bound by his grave clothes.

Most Christians have been told to be suspicious of their hearts, *even after* coming to Christ. In essence, the message to us from the Church has been, "Your heart is bad, or at best, a mix of good and bad. Therefore, be suspicious of your heart, your motives, your desires." How often have we heard the self-effacing idiom, "You're just a sinner, saved by grace."? Or that "We're 'prone to wander.'"?

As I talked with my friends who trusted Jesus, I asked the question: "Even after becoming a Christian, have you been told that your heart is:

   °   totally good and pure,
   °   not at all good and pure,
   °   or a mix of good and bad?"

Some of those interviewed, even though they had been Christians for years, were still believing that their hearts were a "mix of good and bad."

More revealing were some responses to the question, "On a scale of 1- 10 ('ten' being 'totally good and pure'), how good/pure do you feel your heart is?" Some of these deeply serious Christians responded with a less than favorable view of their redeemed hearts. Any answer less than "ten" would indicate a misunderstanding of the thoroughly miraculous work Jesus has already accomplished in them. And it's not their fault. It's the message they've been given. Why are these good people still feeling their hearts are bad in some way—that the deepest part of them is still dirty, marred or unacceptable?

What this message is *not*

Please know that I am clearly not speaking of a self-constructed, self-initiated goodness on our part. We were not born good: God must make us so. We once *were* rebellious towards God and our hearts *were* deceitfully wicked. We once *were* incapable of living and loving like Christ. Any honest person can see that human nature, apart from Christ's radical intervention, is not capable of living from the standard (kind or scope) of love that Jesus sets before us. Without regeneration (radical interior transformation), we can only produce human love, but not the very love of Christ.

Further, when I try to help a follower of Jesus see that his heart is now good, I'm *not* offering a self-help, feel-good seminar on how to actualize his inner light. I'm simply advocating the revolutionary and penetrating work of Christ in the heart that occurs when a person says 'yes' to Jesus. The language we use to talk about ourselves and others betrays our theology, for better or worse; and the version of Christianity that is so pervasive today has done such great damage to our sense of identity. This is why it's necessary to provide a better, more accurate language about ourselves and our wholly new identity as God's sons and daughters.

This message of radical change is exactly what we need, yet we are being given a dangerously distorted version of what actually happened to us. Because of this distortion and anemic teaching concerning what Jesus has actually accomplished in our inmost being, there are many of us who are serious about Jesus yet still captive to shame, guilt, and spiritual pressure tactics.

The gospel of duty, shame and pressure

> Question: "In your experience going to church, have you felt *pressure to be good*, or *freedom to be holy?"*
>
> Cindy, from Hartford: "I don't know that I would call it pressure, but a definite assertion/admonition that as a Christian, I should be behaving a certain way. I don't believe that I have ever heard (in church, at least) that I am holy."

Today's Church preaches a partial, and therefore weakened, anemic gospel. The Gospel has been reduced to: get forgiven—go to heaven. You've been pardoned, but now it's your job to be a "good Christian" and keep your nose clean until Heaven. What starts with grace ends in *pressure* to be good. (Just get people to do the right thing.) The Christian life soon becomes about acting like a good Christian (religious duty) so that you don't disappoint God or those around you. The externals (behavioral expectations) become more important than internal realities (the new resources of your heart). Even good practices such as serving others, worship, ministry and kindness become religious obligations, rather than the overflow of a new heart that is now genuinely for others and for God.

Here's what one Christian discovered about the emptiness of living from religious duty and obligation:

> I was a faithful Christian. I went to church every week and joined the men's ministry—even went on a mission trip to Bulgaria. I want to say I was living for God, but I was living more out of duty and obligation. It was the 'wanting to do the right thing' type of living. On the outside I was the model Christian. However, I had a nagging sense of 'there is something more,' but I could not identify what the 'more' was.[3]

Any "gospel" that *pressures* people to be good inevitably brings shame; because 'good enough' is never good enough. How do we recognize the gospel of duty and pressure, and therefore, shame? This false gospel comes with the following message: "You're not doing enough, you're not spiritual enough, committed enough, selfless enough." It's the "not enough" gospel and it is often called "sanctification." And how can you argue with that? Don't you want to grow spiritually? Shouldn't we serve, become more "Christ-like," be committed to the mission? Here's a troubling question, though: How can you *ever* know when enough is enough?

> When you've read your Bible enough?
> Shared your faith enough?
> Been committed enough?
> Love God enough?

In order to meet the expectation of sanctification, is spiritual growth something we must try harder at, doubling our efforts in order to be more like Christ?

The bait and switch gospel

We say people can come into the Kingdom through grace, but once they're in, we switch from grace to duty, obligation, and pressure. Though we preach that you can't contribute a thing to your own salvation and that it's all God's gift for you, once you're "safe" however, you'd better keep up and step up. This fallacy is why Paul had to be pointedly firm with God's family in Galatia when he said: "Are you so foolish? After beginning with the Spirit, are you now trying to attain your goal by *human effort*?" In today's distorted Christianity, you can come in under God's power, but once you're in the door, it's about *your* effort to make this thing work. Grace dissolves into exertion. And because you can never do enough, exertion soon turns to shame: "I know I'm supposed to be serving, loving, thinking pure thoughts, but I just can't. It goes well for a while, then I blow it... again." Soon, shame turns into resignation: "I no longer *want* to try harder. I feel like giving up." And God asks the Church, "Why do you turn my glory into shame?!"

CHAPTER TWO

The heart is his mission

(Why the heart has to be the focus of Jesus' mission)

"What is in our 'heart' matters more than
anything else for who we become …"
– Dallas Willard, *Renovation of the Heart*[4]

"I will give you a new heart…"
– *Ezekiel 36:26*

W̶hat if you went to your doctor because for two months you'd been experiencing stomach pains that would come and go? After examining you, your doctor says that you need to be on an antacid medication for acid reflux disease, and that some changes in your diet should be made. A month later, after faithfully taking the medication for reflux, your pain has continued, with little to no relief. You return to the doctor who decides to increase your medication dosage and add another medication, reminding you to avoid certain foods. Another month and one-half goes by and the pain is becoming unbearable. You return again to the doctor, who recommends you see a gastrointestinal specialist. The specialist decides to do an endoscopy where she can use a tiny camera to view the lining of your stomach and upper GI tract by inserting a small tube down into your throat. When you wake up from the procedure, the specialist tells you the real problem: you have Stage Four stomach cancer.

How do you feel about your doctor who kept managing your symptoms, but didn't go after the disease … until it was perhaps too late? Angry? Misled? Of course, many doctors are competent and want to see the patient healed and well. But assumptions, preconceptions and pressures can lead to misguided decisions—and this is true of any arena of life where critical thinking is needed. For too long, the Church has been managing symptoms and missing the cure. We've made the behavioral externals (even good ones) the point, attempting to manage them in order to get people to act like Christians. In the process, the heart has been missed, and the heart is what Jesus is after: "Man looks at the outward appearance, but the LORD looks at the heart." (I Sam. 16:7)

Rescue the heart

Albert Einstein said in 1948 that "The true problem lies in the hearts and thoughts of men. It is not a physical but an ethical one … What terrifies us is not the explosive force of the atomic bomb, but the power of the wickedness of the human heart."[5] – Albert Einstein, 1948. Any honest person knows the malignant self-absorption they are capable of apart from God's transforming intervention. Who of us has loved equally and unselfishly all who are within our reach? Have we unreservedly given the same quality of love for our enemies that we do for those we really like? Who has loved God with the continuous affection of a whole heart? Do we wake up trusting God, or distracted with the cares of the unfolding day? Can we say as Jesus did, that "I only do what I see my Father doing" or do we set our day's agenda on our own terms? The possibility of even Christians living an essentially God-less life, or day, or week cannot be denied; and godlessness or goodness finds its roots in the interior recesses of human personality—within the heart itself. Evil is not something "out there." It is something within ... unless Christ's work goes straight to the heart.

Therefore, Christ's work, of necessity, must deal with the heart, the "inside of the cup." As Dallas Willard rightly states: "If we would walk with him, we must walk with him at that interior level [the level of the heart].... He saves us by realistic restoration of our heart to God and then by dwelling there with his Father through the distinctively divine Spirit. The heart thus renovated and inhabited is the only real hope of humanity on earth."[6] Notice that salvation is a rescuing of the heart, for when you rescue the heart you rescue the person.

Writing on the heart

Each follower of Jesus is a poe'ma—a living poem or letter written by God— says the apostle Paul: "... You are a letter from Christ, the result of our ministry, written not with ink but with the Spirit of the living God, not on tablets of stone but on tablets of *human hearts*." So where does the Author and Completer of our faith do his writing? Isn't it upon tablets of the heart? "I will put my law in their minds and write it *on their hearts,*" God says through the prophet Jeremiah. There is something so central about the heart in God's plan of salvation, that Christ makes it a fundamental location of our union with him, so that "Christ may *dwell in your hearts* through faith." It is where God has put the Spirit of his Son: "…God sent the Spirit of his Son into our hearts..." (Gal. 4:6) The redeemed heart is where God has made himself available. In fact, it is where we meet with him when we pray. As Theophan the Recluse said, "Find a place *in your heart* and speak there with the Lord. It is the Lord's reception room."[7]

What is meant by the "heart?"

Contrary to popular culture's view, the heart is *not* the emotional or feeling side of us. Popular culture tends to think of the heart as the sentimental part of us. (Think of *Hallmark* cards.) Biblically speaking, our feelings can *express* what is going on in our hearts, but the heart is much more than feelings. According to the Scriptures, the heart or human spirit is the core of our personality—the true and deepest self. It is also where reason, understanding, and conscience are located[8]. We often think that we only perceive with our minds, yet we can "see" with our hearts. In fact, the heart is the hub that governs all other parts of the self—including the mind, thoughts, feelings, the body and the soul. The function of the heart is "to organize our life as a whole…" says Willard. This description of the self is very much a "systems" way of thinking about life, much like the multiple systems of the human body that cannot function without a healthy heart that effectively pumps blood throughout. An airplane cannot fly in a storm without a properly-functioning navigational system, or it will crash. The heart or human spirit is the navigational system for the rest of the human personality: If it goes wrong, then everything else does as well.

Willard goes on to say that the *redeemed* heart organizes our life around God himself.[9]   The unredeemed heart would organize a person's

energies around any number of things: fear, control, shame, mistrust. The
unredeemed heart is on a desperate search for life, but continues to drive the
person to places that cannot give life. We are thirsty by nature, yet apart
from receiving a new heart, we will go to wells that cannot satisfy our thirst.

It is also true that our real and settled convictions are formed in our
hearts. Our deepest convictions—what we really believe about God—are
formed in the heart: "For it is *with your heart* that you *believe* and are
justified…" (Romans 10:10) For example, the unredeemed heart believes
that God cannot be trusted and that a person must strive, grasp and control in
order to secure an illusion of life. By contrast, the new and redeemed heart
sees the world as saturated through with God's good kingdom, believes that
our Father's heart towards us is actually good, and that we ourselves can live
good, whole, and holy lives in his care. This is why even the doubting and
feeble Christian can say with relief, "My heart *does* trust God's care! I can
now trust and enjoy my Father's good heart the way Jesus trusted him and
enjoyed him."

If the heart (spirit) is not right, all the other parts of the self are not
right. As goes the heart, so goes our bodies, our minds and our souls. Each
part of the human personality is contingent upon the health of our heart.
There is no healthy mind without a healthy heart; no healthy soul without a
healthy heart; and no healthy body without a healthy heart. It's obvious now
why Jesus' saving work has to deal with the heart above all else: the health,
wholeness and holiness of our lives depends upon the health, wholeness and
holiness of our hearts!

Returning to our heart's desire

"There stood his heart's desire, huge and real, the golden Lion, Aslan himself … …"[10]

Long before he arrived in person, Scripture foretold the mission of Jesus: "I will give you a new heart and put a new spirit in you …" (Ezek. 36:26)   The prophet Jeremiah voices the mission of Jesus as well: "*I will give them a heart to know me*, that I am the LORD. They will be my people, and I will be their God, for they will *return to me with all their heart*." (Jer. 24: 7). The history of God's people has sadly demonstrated that it is not possible for us to return to God with all our heart if that heart doesn't *want* to return to God. This is why he says, "I will give them a heart to know me …" God must give us back the heart we lost at the Fall so that we may return to him.

To return to God with a new heart is to return to the life we most truly desire.   The Christian now wants God more than anything—in spite of his contrary actions, doubts, or false convictions—for he now has a heart *for* God. He may be choosing old convictions and habits that deny his new desires, yet the externals can no longer dictate the internal realities: He is a new creature with a rescued and redeemed heart. So when we speak of "salvation," we must speak of it beyond mere terms of forgiveness. Salvation is a rescuing of the heart, and therefore, the entire person.

Is the message of the new heart a new teaching?

Centuries ago, Martin Luther declared the reality of the new heart: "For faith through the merit of Christ obtaineth the Holy Spirit, which Spirit doth *make us new hearts*, doth exhilarate us, doth excite and enflame our heart, that it may do those things willingly which the law of love commandeth."[11]
Notice that the renovation of our inner being or heart enables us to do what we could not before: we can now follow the command of love *willingly*—without spiritual pressure or strong-arming. Church leaders no longer need to beat the commitment drum week after week to get God's people to act. Sermon-series driven by a need to fill volunteer slots and stir up the crowds aren't necessary. When we draw attention to the new desires of a believer's good heart, we no longer need to coax and cajole, for the new-hearted soul wants to serve! We now start with the assumption that the redeemed person *wants* to follow God. What the law commands, the good heart now wants!

Andrew Murray, eighteenth-century pastor and author and first president of the YMCA, recognized that the central promise of the New Covenant "is a heart delighting in God's law..."[12] Therefore, it is a lie when the believer is told that he doesn't love God enough or want to do his will. Though love is clearly demonstrated in action, it is unhelpful and quite harmful to live from an on-going assumption that "I don't love God enough." It is disheartening and dismisses the new internal reality—a heart that now has the very love of Jesus for his Father residing within!

God, in fact, has given us his own goodness: a purity that is natural to him may now be natural to us. The Eighteenth–century preacher, Jonathan Edwards, reminded us that God regenerates our hearts, so that we share in the divine goodness of God: "The first effect of the power of God in the heart in regeneration, is to *give the heart a divine taste or sense*; ... to cause it to have a relish of the loveliness and sweetness of the supreme excellency of the divine nature."[13]   It's not that we are now gods; rather, we have been made internally radiant with a new purity and wholeness. We have not simply put on a robe or outer garment of righteousness—a layer of goodness covering up a horrible mess. Rather, we have been *made* righteous, at the deepest level of human personality.

More recently, J.I. Packer, whom *Time* magazine listed as one of the top 25 most influential evangelicals in America, describes our regeneration as, "the spiritual change wrought in the heart of man by the Holy Spirit in which his/her inherently sinful nature is changed so that he/she can respond to God in Faith, and live in accordance with His will (Matt. 19:28; John 3:3,5,7; Titus 3:5). It extends to the whole nature of man, altering his governing disposition, illuminating his mind, freeing his will, and renewing his nature." He goes on to say that, "The regenerate man has forever ceased to be the man he was; his old life is over and a new life has begun; he is a new creature in Christ, buried with him out of reach of condemnation and raised with him into a new life of righteousness." (See Rom. 6:3-11; II Cor. 5:17; Col. 3:9-11)[14]

Why would God give us a new heart, yet not a *good* one? Isn't it true that what God gives must be good and pure, by default? How could he give something of neutral value? Doesn't he give that which is good and holy, most alive, most representative of his own Son's heart? Because he gives us his own goodness, our new hearts must now be considered good and holy.

Can secular people be "good?"

All this raises a troubling question: Can a person who has not trusted Christ for life and forgiveness be called "good" in any sense? We all know people who do not claim any allegiance to Christ who do kind things for others, love their families and are concerned for the welfare of others. Can their motives or actions be called "good"? The answer lies in this: "good" compared to what? To whom? Is this to be measured by each person's own conception of what goodness is, or is there a constant against which we can define goodness? Wouldn't it be more comforting to know that there is a constant against which goodness can be evaluated, rather than a sliding scale no one can pin down?

Any thoughtful person who considers the moral, intellectual, relational and cultural condition of the world, or his own behavior and leanings, must come to one conclusion: we are not what we were meant to be. Something happened to us ... in us. Something was lost in us. Perhaps by human standards of goodness a non-Christian can be good, but goodness must always be based upon standards Jesus himself established by the way he loved and related to his Father and people around him. Goodness has been radically defined in the life and person of Jesus. Therefore, if un-regenerated hearts (and all that flows from them) could be considered good, then Christ died and was raised for no reason. Rescue would look quite silly, like an ambulance showing up for an accident scene, only to realize that the scene was a movie set with fake blood and actors. There's nothing really wrong there, so why send an emergency response team? Why send in your own son at the certain risk of his own life? Or it is like unnecessary surgery performed on a healthy person. If disease and harm were absent, there would have been no need to remove our old hearts (which produced death in us) and thoroughly replace them with good and pure hearts (which give life).

God sends in his son, our First Responder, not so that we can simply behave like Jesus; but so that we can have his heart. Remember, it has never been about good behavior: It has always been about the interior health and leanings of the spirit/heart. From the heart springs death or life, pure waters or putrid streams. Even a stream that appears to be clear—so that you can see down to the pebbles below—can contain microorganisms that can make you sick. Outward signs do not always indicate inward realities.

Calling people "good" or "bad" based upon external behaviors isn't helpful. Appearances are not guaranteed indicators of what is going on within. If our indicators are simply externals, then there are a lot of "good people" in hell, and a lot of "bad people" in heaven. The Scriptures indicate something wholly different: only re-created people go to heaven. Only those who have received the gift of a new heart from Jesus and his Father are able to be considered truly good because, through surgery, they have inherited the goodness of the Son.

In fact, Jesus makes an assumption that exteriors proceed from interior realities; fruit proceeds from root. To those obsessed with right behavior, he said, "Blind Pharisee! First clean the inside of the cup and dish, and then the outside also will be clean." (Matt. 23:26) Notice how hopeful this is. Exterior goodness will follow when interior goodness is recognized and nourished. As C.S. Lewis reminds us, when you put second things first, you lose both first and second things; but when you put first things first, you gain first and second things. When you put interior goodness first (by means of a new heart), you also get true and healthy exterior holiness as a natural outflow. Yet, when you do not put the new heart as first importance, you lose both the heart and a true demonstration of outward holiness. In this case, you typically end up with a Pharisee, or someone trying really, really hard to be good in his own strength—a shame-filled, defeated Christian. This is where many Christian communities are today.

A better way to connect with God (The old way doesn't work)

The New Covenant (or new way of relating to God) is chiefly concerned with an interior goodness rather than external codes of righteousness. What does the Bible say about this better way to relate to God? How does the reality of a new heart affect our relationship with God and others? For now, we'll look at the way it affects our life with God. Later, we'll discuss the new heart's implications for community.

Because of the gift of our new heart, we've moved away from one way of relating to God—to a better way of relating to him:

From our ability to obey—to Jesus' ability to obey:

Before Jesus comes onto the scene, God's people were not able to keep up their end of the vows: They 'broke covenant." So God had to establish a different way of relating to him that was based on something he does, his ability to come through: "The time is coming," declares the Lord, "when I will make a new covenant with the house of Israel and with the house of Judah. It will not be like the covenant I made with their forefathers ... because they broke my covenant ... This is the covenant I will make with the house of Israel after that time," declares the Lord. "I will put my law in their

minds and write it on their hearts." (Jer. 31: 31, 32, 33) The New Covenant
is a relationship of the heart. Andrew Murray once said, "Through the whole
of the Old Covenant there was always one trouble: man's heart was not right
with God. In the New Covenant the evil is to be remedied. It's central
promise is a heart delighting in God's law..."[15]

The old way of relating is useless and harmful and must be
discarded: "By calling this covenant 'new,' [Jesus] has made the first one
obsolete..." (Heb. 8:13) "For if there had been nothing wrong with that first
covenant, no place would have been sought for another." (Heb. 8:7) The old
way of relating to God didn't work. Under the old system, people were
simply not able to keep the law: they kept 'breaking covenant' with God.
Therefore, an altogether different way of relating to God had to be
established. A relationship could no longer be based upon our ability to
obey, but had to be based upon Jesus' ability to obey. Jesus obeyed on our
behalf. Even more hopeful is that Jesus' ability to obey is now ours. His
will, his integrity of heart, his relentless conformity to his Father's will now
resides in our inmost being.

From outward behavior—to internal goodness:
From outward obedience to law (acting right, trying to be good) to an inward
inclination towards goodness. The law is now written on our hearts— It has
now become internalized. (Gal.5:4. Also Heb. 8:10,13; Jer. 31:33) The new
goodness and purity on the inside can now flow outward. Paul calls his
friends in his letter to the Hebrews, "Holy brothers." (Heb. 3:1). He is
assuming his friends bear a new purity and character.

J. Oswald Sanders declares our new internal goodness when he says, "The New Covenant is written on the fleshly [meaning tissues] tablets of the heart. Under its terms, the desire and ability to do God's will are incorporated into the believing man's *inmost being*. It becomes his second nature, the very spring of his choice and desires ... With his Master he is now able to say, 'I delight to do Thy will, O my God.'"[16]

From striving to be good—to reliance on God's Spirit producing his own fruit within us:

From the outset of this new relationship, Paul had to warn one of his church families to stay true to this new way of relating: "Are you so foolish? After beginning with the Spirit, are you now trying to attain your goal by human effort?" (Gal. 3:3) Discipleship is now God's work in us: "...for it is God who works in you to will and to act according to his good purpose." (Phil. 2:13)

From right religious behavior (observing the law)—to confidence in God:

"Did you receive the Spirit by observing the law, or by believing what you heard? Are you so foolish? After beginning with the Spirit, are you now trying to attain your goal by human effort?" (Gal. 3:2-3) We are now justified (right with God) by faith (trust, confidence), not by right behavior: "For we maintain that a man is justified by faith apart from observing the law." (Rom. 3:28) We have died to the law and been released from the law. (Rom. 7:4-6) Trust and confidence in God's capabilities replaces self-righteousness.

From prisoners to the law—to free sons and daughters:
"Before this faith came, we were held prisoners by the law, locked up until faith should be revealed … Now that faith has come, we are no longer under the supervision of the law." (Gal. 3:23, 25) Relationships founded upon law (codes of right behavior) can only lead to one becoming the slave to the other's expectations. We've moved from slaves to sons and daughters: "So you are no longer a slave, but a son; and since you are a son, God has made you also an heir." (Gal. 4: 7) "It is for freedom that Christ has set you free. Stand firm, then, and do not let yourselves be burdened again by a yoke of slavery." (Gal 5:1)

From a dead heart (and therefore body, mind, and soul)—to an alive heart (and therefore body, mind and soul):
"As for you, you were dead in your transgressions and sins, in which you used to live … But because of his great love for us, God, who is rich in mercy, made us *alive* with Christ even when we were dead in our transgressions." We are now both dead and alive: dead to all the wrong and destructive modes of living and alive to God and all the life-giving patterns of living. (Ephesians 2:1, 4-5) A person is either under law or the Spirit. One kills the heart, the other gives life: "He has made us competent as ministers of the new covenant—not of the letter [law] but of the Spirit; for the letter kills, but the Spirit gives life." (2 Cor. 3:6)

From borrowed righteousness—to actual righteousness:
The Old Covenant system of sacrifices could not do two things: It couldn't take away a person's sin or wash the guilt away. The Old Covenant sacrifices could only lend the person a temporary and outward righteousness:

"The blood of goats and bulls and the ashes of a heifer sprinkled on those who are ceremonially unclean sanctify them so that they are outwardly clean. How much more, then, will the blood of Christ, who through the eternal Spirit offered himself unblemished to God, cleanse our consciences from acts that lead to death, so that we may serve the living God."   "The law ... can never, by the same sacrifices repeated endlessly year after year, make perfect those who draw near to worship. If it could, would they [the sacrifices] not have stopped being offered? For the worshippers would have been cleansed once for all, and would no longer have felt guilty for their sins." "...because it is impossible for the blood of bulls and goats to take away sins." (Heb. 10: 1,2,3,4) Any system of behavior-management can never deal with sin or with guilt.

Under the old way of relating to God, the worshippers borrowed righteousness through the sacrificial system, but it never really *made* them righteous. The old way couldn't take away their sins, or make them feel less guilty. Only the work of Christ's self-sacrifice made it possible to relate to God without guilt; to remove sin as the dominant force in a person's life.

Why God *became* sin

Why does Jesus have to "*become* sin" for us, as Scripture says, rather than merely bearing our sin or suffering for our sin? The disease and dis-ease of sin had to be cured. One of the early Church Father's declared that "what is not assumed cannot be healed." —What is not taken-upon or shouldered or borne by Jesus cannot be transformed. Jesus had to experience each dimension of our existence in order to turn it back to God. If we are to be free of sin's power and shame, Jesus had to take upon himself sin and shame;

so that as he overwhelmed sin by his obedience, we also could be made well and made holy.

The Cross and Resurrection are not religious symbols or metaphors for forgiveness. Something actual and concrete took place on our behalf. A literal exchange took place: "God made him who had no sin *to be sin* for us, so that in him we might become the righteousness of God." (2 Cor. 5:21) During this exchange, Jesus took on a nature that wasn't familiar to him (sin) and we took on a nature that wasn't familiar to us (righteousness). In this exchange, we became the very goodness of God. On the Cross, Jesus absorbed the toxin of sin—and the shame that accompanies it—into his own body. He died to all that is unholy and diseased. Through his rebirth and resurrection, God's original intent for us was restored. Jesus rescued our life and our intended glory by overwhelming the dark and the unholy with purity and power. By "accepting Christ" we decided to die with him and what he died to—to sin and shame—and to rise up into a new cleanness. Said another way, we died to our old, diseased hearts, and now enjoy the resurrection of a new and pure heart—founded upon a guilt-free, shame-free purity.

There is more to this Story than we've been told.

CHAPTER THREE

Recovering the rest of the Gospel

(the heart re-created)

"Man finds it hard to get what he wants, because he does not want the best;

God finds it hard to give, because he would give the best,

and man will not take it."

– George MacDonald, *Unspoken Sermons*[17]

I ran aground in a harbour town

Lost the taste for being free

Thank God He sent some gull-chased ship

To carry me to sea

– Bruce Cockburn, *All the Diamonds*

What we're not being told

M uch of what passes for the "gospel" these days is a message of exhortation without regeneration—preaching that excludes the New Covenant reality of a transformed heart. (Or more accurately, preaching that is grossly unaware of this transformation having already occurred.)

Christian preachers and pundits try to get people to behave like Christians and to be 'more like Christ.' Surely it is good and right for us to be like Jesus, doing the things he did, having the same ruling passions he does. However, you can't possibly reproduce the works of Jesus without living from a fundamentally transformed self. You cannot also reproduce the works of Jesus or even live from the vitality of Christ if you don't *know* that you are a fundamentally transformed person. This is where most Christians are today: they simply *don't know* they've already been substantially changed (or "regenerated").

We simply aren't being told that something deep and central has been restored to us. We have a "gospel" that offers only a fraction of God's redemptive work for us. This gospel is primarily about getting our sins forgiven and hoping for heaven: "Get right with God and do your best to be good." As Dick Staub says in his insightful book, *The Culturally Savvy Christian,* we have an impoverished "faith community satisfied with a *reunion* with God and future hope of heaven, but without the radical spiritual, intellectual, creative, relational, and moral wellness that comes through the *restoration* of God's image now."[18]   That restoration of God's image occurs foremost as a restoration of our deep core, our central identity … our hearts. With some exceptions here and there, the message of a restored heart simply isn't being told to the masses of Christians in local churches. Even more organic and less institutionalized forms of the Body are susceptible to a gospel of exhortation without regeneration; for we carry our theological assumptions with us wherever we go.

Disabling Assumptions

The message we too often hear as Christians is, "You're a prisoner who's been pardoned, but you're still the same person you've always been. Try harder not to sin. You're heart is suspect and prone to wander, but try harder not to wander and stray." That's why we have 'accountability groups'—brothers and sisters policing us in order to help us manage our sin. The assumption behind 'accountability' as practiced today assumes all the wrong things about the believer's heart. Author Wayne Jacobsen was sent a cartoon of Jesus inviting people to come to him. The caption read, "Come to me, all you who are weary and heavy-laden, and I will give you an accountability group." Accountability is so ... *Old* Covenant.

We pressure Christians to be holy, and then tell them they're not. We start with a negative: "You're job is to become like Christ, but good luck, because you're clearly not like Christ: You're too selfish, too needy and too committed to your own happiness." Because we don't start with the believer's new heart—with the goodness that is now theirs because they trust Christ—we wound people with a shame-based message: "You weren't enough to please God before you became a Christian, and you're still not enough to please him even now."

Accusation and condemnation have become the Church's primary tools for manipulating transformation. (By the way, these are the same weapons that the Devil, appropriately called "The Accuser," brings against God's family.) Shame is *not* God's method for change. In fact, Scripture shouts, "Therefore, there is now *no condemnation* for those who are in Christ Jesus." Not a shred of accusation.

But doesn't Jesus use harsh words when he speaks to the Pharisees or when he rebukes Peter? Don't his words sound accusing in these instances? First, I think it would help to offer one way to understand "accusation." Whenever Jesus exposes something in a person, such as self-deception, spiritual arrogance, or any destructive belief, it is so that the person may live free of it. After all, he wants us well and whole. Therefore, if Jesus ever sounds accusing, it is an act of mercy and rescue.

Second, "accusation" may be understood as a false indictment—alleging something untrue about a person's character—claiming that the person's essential nature is evil. Accusation is a defamation of the heart—calling the central nature of a person "bad," when in fact, that individual's heart and intent are truly good. The Pharisees accused Jesus of being demon-possessed—slandering his heart—when, in fact, there was no one more holy and full of goodness than he! And the Church is carrying on the tradition of the Pharisees when it continues to teach that the believer's heart is still criminal and suspect.

Pressure doesn't help

Scripture indicates that we began this journey 'justified' by grace through faith, and not external rule-keeping. Pressure to be good doesn't help. If law-keeping and spiritual pressure couldn't make us righteous to begin with, why would we allow ourselves to come under that very burden of shame and spiritual futility again? It's like being rescued after falling through the ice, then jumping back into the icy abyss again. Yet it's the distorted gospel we've been given, and the false message our leaders were also given. It's a distortion and disability that's been handed down to us through generations.

The message of exhortation translated today says, "You're not doing enough of this; or you're doing too much of that:" "You're too selfish, not committed to your marriage, not serving enough ..." Exhortation becomes an attempt to manage (or manipulate) people's behavior by pressure and guilt, rather than urging them to release the good stored up in their heart through Christ's work in them. As Larry Crabb pointed out in his ground-breaking book, *Connecting*, discipleship is about *releasing* a goodness now present within the believer because of Christ's redemptive work in them.[19]

I must state again that this goodness is *not* natural to humanity: It is only God-given—given to us at the moment we placed our confidence in him. Yet it is a supernatural purity that goes unrecognized and unrealized in churches everywhere.

After years of hearing a message of accusation, a Christian succumbs to a disabling and toxic view of his heart. Worse, he begins to believe that his heart is not, in fact, good, even as one who walks with Jesus. He comes to suspect his heart and its motives, policing his every thought and intent.

Having said that, let me be clear that not all thoughts that pass through the Christian's mind are good, nor all his desires pure, nor every action holy. We still have the capacity to sin (to live from the old self), yet a sinful *nature* is no longer ours: It is no longer our core identity. Goodness and purity is our new character, no matter how deeply buried or ignored. We are new and wholly different. Theologians have typically called this, 'regeneration.' We have lost this most basic assumption that Scripture itself makes.

What exactly is new?

How many times have we heard that we are "a new creation" in Christ and yet felt a vague sense of dismay and confusion? Perhaps even disqualification? "I know I'm supposed to be a new creation but I really don't feel any different. There must be something wrong with me." So what exactly changed when we came to Christ? What became new? How are we "new creations"?

For centuries, theologians have rightly upheld the idea of "regeneration," or the drastic transformation of heart Christ brings about. Sometimes, this is called the "new birth," a spiritual re-creation of our deepest self. It therefore includes a re-creation of the heart. This restored heart is exactly what Paul means when he says, "Therefore, if anyone is in Christ, he is a new creation; the old has gone, the new has come!" (2 Cor. 5:17) We should "put off the old self ... and put on the new self." (Eph. 4:22-24)

That 'new self' is a new heart given to us at conversion. Our radical goodness is an already-established fact, a gift given when we trusted Jesus. The new heart is the fulfillment of God's promise to us in Ezekiel 36:26 and Jeremiah 31: 31-34.

"I will give you a new heart and put a new spirit in you ..." (Ezekiel 36:26)

Jesus literally removes our old, corrupted heart and gives us a new and good heart in its place. By 'remove,' we don't mean that the old self is gone for good. (This doesn't occur until the next life.)   However, it does mean that the old, rebellious heart has been removed from our center—dethroned and disempowered. It has been sidelined. A quite substantial and dramatic shift has occurred inside of us. This change in us is central to Christ's work in us, and everything that follows in our journey depends upon understanding it.

The Church today largely has missed the message of a regenerated life today. What happened to the Biblical idea of *regeneration*? It's been replaced almost completely by a Justification Gospel which says, "You're off the hook, but are the same person you've always been. So don't blow it." Yet Jesus points to this supernatural rebirth when he tells Nicodemus that he must be "reborn from above." Nicodemus must experience a kind of renewal that can only be described as super-natural. Dallas Willard, in *Renovation of the Heart*, says, "The spiritual renovation … that comes from Jesus is nothing less than an invasion of natural human reality by a supernatural life 'from above.'"[20]

But *what* got 'reborn' or 'regenerated?' Our outlook on life? Our worldview? Our attitudes? Our sense of worth? Are not these all filtered through the heart? Can we possibly receive a new life without first receiving a new heart from which those attitudes, outlooks, and aliveness flow? Doesn't God's life flow from the heart, as the poet David insists, when he warns us to watch over our hearts—the wellspring of life within us? Yet it is not as if our hearts were merely given an upgrade or a new coat of paint. This wouldn't do. In fact, a mere sprucing up of the old would not be sufficient. God did not come to tinker with or improve our old nature, but to wholly replace it with something remarkable.[21] As C.S. Lewis reminds us, "God became man to turn creatures into sons; not simply to produce better men of the old kind but to produce a new kind of man."

We're not simply "saved" because we're forgiven. You don't lift a prisoner's sentence, release him, then leave him as he his. You restore him so that he can function in a wholly new way, lest he repeat his crimes and return to his criminal nature. Pardon (forgiveness) is not enough. He must be made "a new kind of man," as Lewis says. The way God "saves" us and makes us new kinds of men and women is precisely by giving us a new and clean heart: "He saved us *through* the washing of rebirth and renewal by the Holy Spirit…" (Tit. 3:5) The cry of the Old Covenant songwriter, David, has now been answered: "Create in me a clean heart, O God, and renew a right spirit within me." (Ps. 51:10) We may now enjoy a clean heart and a right spirit—because that new goodness is now fixed within us.

A heart full of wine

The old self was so beyond repair, beyond salvaging, so thoroughly unresponsive to God, that it had to be utterly *replaced*. After all, you cannot put the new wine into an old wineskin, or both will be ruined. You need a thoroughly new wineskin. You can also not sew a new patch on an old garment or it will tear:

No one sews a patch of unshrunk cloth on an old garment, for the patch will pull away from the garment, making the tear worse. Neither do men pour new wine into old wineskins. If they do, the skins will burst, the wine will run out and the wineskins will be ruined. No, they pour new wine into new wineskins, and both are preserved. (Matt. 9:16-17)

We are the new wineskins. More specifically, our new hearts are the new wineskins, now filled with the intoxicating new wine of the indwelling Spirit of Christ himself.

When the message of the new heart is lost or given no practical significance even if acknowledged, what develops is exhortation without regeneration—pressure to be holy, with little hope of becoming holy. How can one become holy when one is consistently told that one is not holy, or that one's heart is a suspicious mix of bad and good? "You need to be more loving, but you're not loving … You need to serve more, but you don't really want to … You need to be a better husband, but you'll probably blow it."

Our new supernatural resources and tendencies
We now *want* to do God's will.
We now have a set of good desires that are deeper than any false desires: "For in my inner being I delight in God's law…" (*Paul*, Rom. 7:22) Remember that Luther indicated this when he said, that "it [the new heart] may do those things willingly which the law of love commandeth." These good and holy desires may be buried or denied, but are real and present beneath the surface. These new, Spirit-wrought desires are now our ruling

passions. Discipleship is about releasing and nurturing these new ruling
passions: "And the good in every Christian's soul waiting to be released
beneath all the emotional and selfish rubble is the longing to be relationally
holy, the urge to bless, to turn the other cheek, to live responsibly, to suffer
well, to hope, to rejoice during hard times. And that set of urges, which
controlled every moment of Jesus' life as he lived on earth, has been given to
us in the gospel."[22]

We now have the *power* to love and relate as Jesus did.
The heart is deeper than sentimentality and emotions, though these things
may proceed from the heart. But more accurately, the heart is the ruling
center that governs the other parts of our self. It is the executive epicenter of
human personality, radiating its influence to the mind, body and soul.
Because of Christ, our freshly-created heart has the will and power to govern
us in healthy, God-ward ways. The Holy Spirit has fused his life with our
own and bound the heart of Jesus with ours, in order that his divine power
may freely flow from within us.

We now have a choice.
The only option for goodness and wholeness is by a thorough replacement of
the former nature of a man or woman—and a receiving of a new, glorious,
and truer nature. Without that new nature (new heart), it is impossible to
love with the depth, scope or consistency of Jesus. By trusting the work of
Jesus (his life, death, resurrection and ascension) for our liberation, our
natural capacities have been replaced with super-natural capacities. In any
situation, the follower of Jesus may still choose his old self with its ruling
desires; yet choosing the old nature leads only to madness—like Sisyphus
doomed with the eternal task of pushing a boulder up a hill, only to nearly

reach the top when the boulder escapes him, forcing him to begin all over again. And again. And again. Futility is the nagging ache of religion, for religion requires goodness, yet refuses God's gift of goodness already present in the new heart. In contrast to religious thinking, our present hope for personal transformation comes as we choose to live from our new and radiant heart.

Some might ask: "How do we know that the heart Jesus gave us is thoroughly pure and good, rather than simply a neutral heart—neither good nor bad—but simply new?" My answer is this: Why would God give us a heart, yet not a *good* one? Isn't it true that what God gives must be good and pure in nature? How could he give anything lesser? How could he give something of neutral value? It would be against his very nature to do so. The new heart (new self) he gives is as radically pure as the old one was radically depraved. The work of Christ is a "How much more..." glorious restoration.

Coupled with our need for a better vision of our new hearts is the need to see God's heart in a less suspicious manner. We have some very mistaken ideas about his heart towards us.

God's fierce affection

A number of years ago, the *Associated Press* reported that a young 12-year-old Ethiopian girl had been kidnapped by a group of men. It was not uncommon for young girls to be kidnapped and forced into marriage: "The United Nations estimates that more than 70 percent of marriages in Ethiopia are by abduction, practiced in rural areas where the majority of the country's 71 million people live." After the men beat the young girl for several days, an odd trio of rescuers came to her aid—three lions approached and chased the men away.

The three lions *guarded* the young girl for half a day before her family and the authorities found her. "They stood guard until we found her and then they just left her like a gift and went back into the forest," the police sergeant reported. If the lions hadn't come to her rescue, the girl may have been beaten even longer and possibly raped in order to force her into marriage.[23]

The obvious question is, "Why didn't the lions eat her?" What triggered a rescuing instinct rather than a feeding one? As I read the article, I also found it strange that there were *three* lions—a trinity of fierce-hearted rescuers who left the young girl "like a gift" and faded into the forest. Could these feral rescuers have been three lions in the service of another Lion?

God comes to his loved-ones' rescue with fierce devotion. There's a story about Elisha, a prophet of Israel, that sounds like it is straight out of the latest fantasy novel. The countries of Israel and Aram were at war with each other. Elisha the prophet has just made an enemy out of the king of Aram for spying on him and conveying the king of Aram's battle plans to Israel's king. So the king of Aram sends out a war party to find the prophet. Here's the Scriptural account of what happens next:

When the servant of the man of God [Elisha's servant] got up and went out early the next morning, an army with horses and chariots [the enemy] had surrounded the city. "Oh, my lord, what shall we do?" the servant asked. "Don't be afraid," the prophet answered. "Those who are with us are more than those who are with them." And Elisha prayed, "O LORD, open his eyes so he may see." Then the LORD opened the servant's eyes, and he looked and saw the hills full of horses and chariots of fire all around Elisha. (2 Kings 6: 15-17)

We are still living in a supernatural Story in which God continues to come for his loved ones.

What we *say* we believe

There are the beliefs about God that we say we have, that we're supposed to hold to as good Christians, and there are the beliefs that are underneath all that, the ones that actually rule us. Those deeply-rooted beliefs are the ones that guide us, for better or worse. One of my long-entrenched beliefs has been that God is at best ambivalent towards me; dispassionate and uninterested in my heart and my desires. The accompanying message is: "It doesn't matter what you want or what you think you can offer." Further still, I've often felt God to be the Great Corrector: "Don't do that." "That's not enough." "That's not the right way to do it." I've believed God to be nitpicking my every thought and act. What a terrible view of God—yet one that is not so easy to let go of—because those convictions have been formed and reformed over 42 years—way below the surface of conscious thought.

I have taken God to be "a harsh man" like the master in the parable of the talents. As Dallas Willard says, "In the same way, we demean God immeasurably by casting him in the role of the cosmic boss, foreman or autocrat, whose chief joy in relation to humans is ordering them around, taking pleasure in seeing them jump at his command and painstakingly noting down any failures. Instead we are to be God's friends and fellow workers."[24]

Are we not sought after, pursued and fought for by a strong and surprisingly kind King? Does he not take deep and giddy pleasure in us? Does he not sing over us with foolish affection? Isn't he our lion-hearted rescuer, who comes with the stealth of a ghost and the fierce affection of a protective father? Is his heart not *for* us?

What is God up to in us?

What, in fact, is God's deep desire for us? What does he long to do for us? Is it not much more than forgiveness? In fact, the Gospel is a message of a restored person. People who are not whole cannot wholly give themselves to something. At the Fall, we lost our *selves*, because we gave our hearts away…

Heart equals self.

God wants to restore our hearts to us, to give us back our life and our aliveness. As George MacDonald says, the story of humanity's journey with God is about his longing to give us life, his own: "The whole history is a divine agony to give divine life to creatures. The outcome of that agony … will be radiant life, whereof joy unspeakable is the flower." And, "All the growth of the Christian is the more and more life he is receiving."[25]

The invitation is to "radiant life."

It was God's original intent, from millennia past to give us a radiant, whole life: "Long before he laid down earth's foundations, he had us in mind, had settled on us as the focus of his love, to be made whole and holy by his love." (*The Messege*, Eph. 1:4) As John Eldredge points out, holiness and wholeness must be taken together. Rather than an austere, painful exercise in super-spirituality, holiness is an invitation to wholeness. We cannot be holy unless we are whole, and cannot be whole until we are holy.

Notice that Christian growth is about receiving more life! Jesus indicated that it was a kind of full-hearted life, lived in union with God and all the resources of his Kingdom. Yet, one cannot live full-hearted and substantially restored and still remain under the unkind assumption that one's heart is still marred, dirty or faithless. Restoration also is not likely to occur when a person believes that God's primary goal is to get them to behave and act like good little Christians "ought." That yoke of slavery no longer fits God's children.

How can we live a new life if we don't really believe our hearts are treasured and not trampled? Could we even begin to change if we believe

God uses shame to change us or pressures us into spiritual conformity?   If our convictions about both ourselves and him are wrong, we have little hope of a new life.   Is there a better way of thinking about our life in God?   About our hearts?

CHAPTER FOUR

Offering a more hopeful message

(Better assumptions about the Christian's heart)

"If you want to build a ship, don't drum up people together to collect wood
and don't assign them tasks and work, but rather teach them to long for the
endless immensity of the sea."
— Antoine de Saint-Exupery

"Give up your good Christian life and follow Christ."
— Garrison Keilor

What we've been told

The following statements are from well-intended church leaders and
Christians I've listened to over the years. Notice the assumptions about
the heart. No differentiation was made in these messages to distinguish
between the believer with his renewed heart and those who have not yet
chosen new life from Jesus:

"We are *by nature* selfish."

"We are "*just as likely* to sin after becoming a Christian
as we were before becoming one.""

"We're just sinners saved by grace."

"We are prone to wander."

These statements were made to both those who professed Christ and those who did not. A song currently playing on "Christian" radio demonstrates the widespread misunderstanding of the Gospel. The songwriter attempts to reject his old way of life: "Get away 'self.' I don't have room for you anymore." This sounds holy, yet is terribly misguided. Since when is Christianity a rejection of the self? Isn't it more accurate to say that what we are actually rejecting is the *old* self—the former, corrupt heart? Aren't we really crucifying the flesh or old self, dying to our former nature? Denying yourself and taking up your cross is a repudiation of an old way of relating.

Would Jesus initially offer us a new and radiant heart, only to require us to reject it later? Of course not. Yet, Christians are often admonished by well-meaning leaders to reject the self, with no attempt to distinguish between the rejection of the old heart (old self) and the embracing of the new self. We don't die to our new hearts, we die to our old and corrupted nature.

"Grace" is not simply getting off the hook for your sins. Grace is the offer of a new and pure heart; a new capacity and longing for holiness—a new self.

Missing the real problem

A friend and I were reflecting on a sermon we had recently heard in which
the pastor was urging people to be more honest in their relationships and
toward God. The pastor concluded that the reason people (he was speaking
primarily to Christians) are not as honest as they should be was because of a
deep-seated condition: "It's a heart problem," the pastor said.

So, as my friend and I sat smoking cigars (some of my best
conversations have been over a good cigar), I asked him: "What did you
think about the pastor's statement—that it's a "heart problem." Is he right?
While my friend paused to think through it, I asked another question: "Is it a
heart problem or a flesh problem?" As we talked through it, we agreed that it
was, in fact, a struggle with the flesh, or old *self*, *not* with the heart. When I
told my friend that his heart was now pure because of Christ, he immediately
felt a sense of pressure lift from him. Christians may be slow to *live from*
their hearts, but sin is never a "heart problem" in the believer: sin is a flesh
problem. As Christians, we don't reject our hearts: we reject (consider as
dead) our flesh through Christ's cross.

Start with the new heart

What if, rather than pressuring Christians to be good, we told Christians,
"Because you trust Jesus, you have a good heart now, and our job is to help
you nourish and release that goodness."? For example, what if we said:

> "You *do* love God. Look at the ways you've already been
> expressing that. Even your concern that you may not demonstrates

the goodness of your heart."

"You are not a selfish person. You may have acted in some selfish ways, but your heart is really *for* others. Can you believe that is what's most true of you now?"

"You are not a lustful man. Your lust may feel intense, and you've even taken your needs to the wrong places, but I know your heart. That isn't you. Let's find what your truest desires are."

"Your heart is for your children. I see the ways you've moved towards them with affection and patience before. You can love them with that same affection and patience now."

When a woman grasps for control of people and events around her, God might say to her, "I know you're afraid. Bring that to me. I also know that your deepest desire is to trust my care for you, rather than arranging for security on your own terms. Let's walk through this together."

When a man seeks his identity through career or his giftedness, or a pastor can't back away from ministry obligations because it has become his identity, his gracious Father may say to him, "I love your gifts and strengths. You've got a lot to contribute, but I want more for you. And I know that you want more. You will feel most secure when you believe you are, above all, my son whom I am deeply pleased with and love to be around. Feel the honor and strength of being my son." Rather than offering the man condemnation for his false attempts to find value, God points him to the source of his deepest strength and value.

A crippling assumption

Why is it easier to believe you are more likely to sin and to succumb than it is to believe your heart is good and strong? Why do our assumptions about ourselves lean towards the probability of sin rather than holiness? As I was praying for my wife and daughter last night at bedtime, I was praying in way that has become a common practice for me, asking God:

> "Father, help me to move towards my wife and daughter in a way that honors and cherishes them and makes them feel well-pursued, so that they see you as their Lover–King who pursues them and fights for their beauty."

(I pray a bit differently for my son, since a boy's heart needs different things than a woman's or little girl's heart does.) However, as I'm praying for my girls, I heard God break in, saying, "You *do*, Jim. You do pursue them well."

Notice that my assumption as I was praying was that I *wasn't* pursuing them in a way that honored them, or at least not doing it *enough*. This 'not enough' accusation is a discouraging and hopeless assumption I've lived with most of my life, because it distorts my self-perception, preventing me from seeing the good that God has already done in me. "Not enough" condemns the good heart, preventing a person from experiencing the joy of holiness, because they're never enough … of something.

So God broke in while I was praying: "You already do honor them and pursue your wife and daughter well, Jim." Perfectly, of course not. Poorly at times, certainly. But to miss or dismiss the good already present is to miss the very mission of Jesus: He comes to energize and call out the good heart he gave us at salvation.

Doesn't God call us to be 'perfect?'

But doesn't Jesus call us to be perfect? —"Be perfect, therefore, as your heavenly Father is perfect." I've always thought this to be an impossible command. Why would God ask me to love perfectly (always and to the degree that Jesus does), knowing that is not likely, holding me to an impossible standard and then judging me for my inability to keep an impossible standard? The difficulty with this passage is the English version doesn't render the word translated, 'perfect' very well.

The command to be 'perfect' must be interpreted by the preceding context, yet only once have I ever heard a church leader say that. We've always stripped the command of the very context that would help us understand what Jesus meant by 'perfect.'

Jesus has just been describing a love that surpasses the standard of love the crowd had come to expect. For example, Jesus says, "You have heard it was said, 'Love your neighbor and hate your enemy.' But I tell you: Love your enemies and pray for those who persecute you…" He is challenging the expectation that we're to love only those who haven't done us wrong, that only people who treat us well deserve our love. So why are we to love those we are at odds with, or those who are even violently at odds with us? Is it simply the right thing to do, or is there a better reason? Jesus answers that question: Even God, "causes his sun to rise on the evil *and* the good, and sends rain on the righteous *and* the unrighteous." Even wicked people are provided with rain for crops, and sun for warmth. Even those who reject God are still offered his kindness.

Then Jesus reinforces the point and says, "And if you greet only your brothers, what are you doing more than others? Do not even pagans do that?" In other words, our kindness ought to extend beyond normal expectations. God our Father's love widens the circle of those who get his blessings. The scope of our love has now been redefined to include those whom the Father includes in his love. That's why Jesus can say, "Be perfect, therefore, as your heavenly Father is perfect." Perfect how? This passage does not indicate a moral, spotless life without blemish. Rather it urges a perfection or completeness in how we love and relate. The verse would be more accurately translated, "Be complete in love; not leaving anyone out, including your most violent enemies and those you have no use for." For God's love is complete in scope, casting a wide net, leaving no one out of his kindness—even those who want nothing to do with him. Does this imply that because God's love doesn't leave anyone out that all are automatically saved? No. I don't believe in universal salvation by any stretch of the imagination. But is does mean that God moves toward all people with an irrational kindness, even if they reject it.

This more accurate understanding of 'being perfect'—or all-encompassing in the scope of my love—brought relief from guilt and futility. However, one could ask, "Isn't 'completeness in love for all people' still an impossible standard?" Difficult, yes. Impossible, no. Why? Because the pressure is off. The gospel of self-effort and teeth-gritting has been abolished. We now have come under the strength and effort of the Holy Spirit, who releases our new goodness because it is his own supernatural goodness. Holiness is not a bearing-down, self-striving drudgery. Rather, it is an "easy yoke" as Jesus calls his life. Holiness becomes "easy" because being yoked to Jesus' goodness is a relief from spiritual pressure to be good. It is not 'easy,' in the sense of requiring no action or engagement of our strength. We do engage our heart, soul, mind and strength as we live from our new goodness. It is 'easy' because goodness can become natural to us over time. Isn't addiction and the pain of entrenched habits more difficult and more of a burden than the experience of true goodness? Don't we want to be free of those things that pin us down? —Free from false comforters like food and mindless entertainment? —Free from outbursts of anger? — Free from destructive beliefs about God that drive us away from his heart rather than to it? —Free from a lifestyle of joyless striving?

Becoming or releasing?

There is an assumption that sounds holy, but produces a great deal of shame and guilt in the Church today. The assumption is this: "You are to become like Jesus." (Stay with me for a minute, as I unpack this.) We are often admonished to *become* better pray-ers, *become* better husbands, *become* better parents, *become* better servants, *become* better church members; yet the problem with this assumption of "becoming" is that it assumes you are not yet something. For example, "You are not a good enough pray-er. You have not committed yourself to God's will enough. You do not want to love your neighbor." —At least ... *not enough.* Now, of course, we are to become like Jesus. Scripture is clear on that. However, a theology that constantly calls one to become something because it assumes that you are not yet holy, or committed, or trusting, actually denies the reality of your new heart and purity. It denies that a radical change of heart has already occurred.

A better approach to understanding God's dramatic work in us is to assume just the opposite: "You *do* want to serve. You *are* becoming a better spouse. You *are* committed to God's will." Why? Because you have a new heart that now wants what God wants, and has the power to carry it out. Therefore, the job of Christian leadership and community is to help you release your new desires and supernatural capacities in a way that is consistent with your new character and unique calling. The new heart of the believer must be unshackled and given permission to guide us as God intended, for Jesus has made our hearts his center of operations. The heart is a beachhead into all parts of the human personality. That's why the new heart is the "well-spring of life." (Prov. 4:23)

What God assumes

Yet, we can never receive the easy yoke of Jesus if we don't believe our hearts are wholly different than they used to be. Pressure to be good won't get us there. We must operate on a different set of assumptions, because God does. We must assume that the work of the Cross and Resurrection has now given us a leaning toward holiness and no longer toward sin. Our truest

motives are toward goodness. Again, J. Oswald Sanders declares our new
internal goodness when he says,

> "The New Covenant is written on the fleshly [meaning tissues]
> tablets of the heart. Under its terms, the desire and ability to do
> God's will are incorporated into the believing man's inmost being. It
> becomes his second nature, the very spring of his choice and desires
> … With his Master he is now able to say, 'I delight to do Thy will, O
> my God."[26]

When God interacts with his maturing sons and daughters now, he
assumes they want what he wants. He treats them as people who are after his
own heart. Though he's not blind towards the possibility of sin or false
motives, he no longer believes sin is their deepest longing. God assumes that
goodness is now our first nature:

> "And such were some of you; but you were washed, but you were
> *sanctified*, but you were justified in the name of the Lord Jesus
> Christ, and in the Spirit of our God."
> –I Cor. 6:11

> "And by that will, we *have been made holy* through the sacrifice of
> the body of Jesus Christ once for all." – Heb. 10:10

You have been *made* righteous, not simply declared righteous. God
does not look upon you as if you still have a depraved and corrupt heart, but
turns a blind eye and calls you "good." This pretending would be dishonest.

Rather, by binding you to the death and resurrected life of his Son, God has given you a new purity. Your core identity and truest self is now good. You are "dead to sin but alive to God in Christ Jesus." Among other things, this signals a new set of inclinations with the believer. Our desire is now for God and all that he himself desires. We are dead to sin because it need not deceive or sway us any longer. We no longer look to sin and its false promises of life; for we are alive to God. Our life and vitality is in that direction.

Two different sermons

Here's a contrasting list of possible sermon titles that demonstrates the difference between Old Covenant preaching (inappropriate assumptions about the believer) and New Covenant preaching (correct assumptions about the believer):

OLD COVENANT PREACHING	NEW COVENANT PREACHING
"How to Avoid Temptation"	*"Gratifying Your New Purity"*
"The Seven Deadly Sins"	*"You No Longer Want That ... Really."*
"Becoming a Better _____"	*"Learning to Live from the Heart"*
"Just Do It"	*"Released From Pressure"*
"Seduced by Desire"	*"Exploring Your New Appetites"*

The assumptions of Old Covenant preaching are no longer valid. The supremacy of Christ is uniquely demonstrated through the supernatural renovation of our hearts. Therefore, we no longer need messages invariably telling us to avoid sin, or to become a better spouse, more faithful church member, or involved parent. Nor do we need messages that pressure us to serve, or Old Covenant teaching that assumes all our desires are still selfish. Rather, we need a different focus, a different obsession—we need to uncover the rich purity and new passions of our redeemed hearts.

Misunderstanding "conviction"

"But doesn't God convict us of our sins even when we're Christians?" Of course. However, there is a difference between accusation and conviction. Accusation assumes the person's very heart is misguided and corrupted by selfish motive. Accusation is a weapon that proceeds from Old Covenant thinking: "You're sinning because you really are that kind of person."

The opposite of accusation is conviction. Conviction is exposure without condemnation: "Yes, I know you did that, but I am not ashamed of you. You will always be my delight."

God's convicting work is now embedded within a wholly new set of assumptions about us. God assumes there is a new vitality and purity about us because he himself performed the surgery within us. He has disabled our corrupt and former selves and replaced what was diseased, so that we might live with hearts fully alive, so that goodness is now our first-nature. Therefore, whenever God convicts, he exposes something that prevents us from experiencing the thrill of our new regal goodness.

CHAPTER FIVE

Conforming to the hive

(Getting with the program vs. living from the new heart)

"Resistance is futile."
– The Borg Collective, *Star Trek – The Next Generation*
(The Borg are a cyber-race that joins victims to their ranks
through forced assimilation.)

Question: "In your experience going to church, have you felt pressure to be good or freedom to be holy?"

Meredith, from Tampa: "I have felt the pressure to conform in churches. I am not free to be the woman God created me to be. For example, I went to one church, and a group of people ostracized me because I am Jewish. I have been a believer [in Christ] since I was a little girl. [Many Jews have been coming to faith in Jesus.] None of them asked me anything about my relationship with God or made an attempt to get to know me. They called me a 'fake' Christian that 'serves two masters.' I still have no idea why they said that … They use themselves as the measuring stick of goodness against others … In church I feel lonely very often …"

Meredith's story

The following are excerpts from a series of e-mails from a friend who has discovered just how wounding churches are that use control and shame. Here are Meredith's own words:

"I was thinking about recovering a good heart and understanding it. One thing I have noticed about myself is the terrible toll spiritual abuse takes on a person (in churches). Churches deal some terrible and unnecessary blows to a heart out of a desire to control. Not all churches are this way, of course.

Right now, I am trying to recover from a situation like that. I am a young, strong, stable, successful woman. And, I have to say that I am reduced to panic attacks and tears in trying to go to church. I found a nice one, and am soldiering through so I don't miss out on what the church has to offer. But, whew, what a rough time I have, sometimes!

It all comes from having been in a congregation in which I was used terribly, lied to, not allowed to defend myself, and forced to conform in every conceivable way. Even getting away from the congregation was hard. The leader cursed me and cried when I left. I was harassed by the people in the congregation for leaving. In retrospect the whole thing seems ridiculous, because it was. But, it is still something I have to work through a lot. And I am finding that situations like mine are not as uncommon as I once believed."

Meredith goes on to say:

> "One great thing that has come out of this is that my relationship
> with God has flourished and I am getting to know Him more and
> more as a friend and it has been amazing. My relationship has never
> been better with Him, truly.
>
> However, I have lost a lot of friends out of this. When I left my
> congregation, naturally I lost a lot of friends. My remaining friends
> from there (who weren't as involved) do not understand what I am
> going through and neither do the rest of my church-going friends.
> When I share my heart with them, I am met with disbelief and
> judgment and Scriptures having nothing to do with the situation are
> hurled at me like weapons. (As if I have done something to deserve
> to be abused.) They tell me that if I don't go to church I will lose my
> relationship with God. Which I know from experience is bologna!
> Although I have visited a seemingly nice church twice recently....
>
> Since all of this I have reached out to other friends who don't go to
> church and told them what happened and asked them why they don't
> go to church. They have had experiences like mine! And
> unfortunately they have moved to other parts of the country or the
> world, so I don't get to spend time with them excepting brief visits
> here or there. Consequently, I feel so isolated."

When churches don't believe the New Covenant truth that each
believer is given a new heart (and now want to do God's will), those

churches will resort to control and shame as means of persuading and manipulating their people.

Dennis's story

A friend of mine, Dennis, is afraid he may be fired from the church where he's a drummer for the worship band. The reason they could ask him to leave has nothing to do with his abilities as a musician or his desire to serve. The church has instituted the typical church-wide small group mandate, stating that every person on every team needs to be involved in a small group. (You have to love mandated relationships. Contrived community always comes up empty.) It's not enough that everyone on the worship team is being strongly urged to participate in a small group, but they also have to read the same book. Perhaps that means that everyone will be on the same page when they're done reading the book. (Getting people on the same page usually means that disagreeing with the leadership is discouraged. Can you smell autocratic "unity" here?) Notice the pressure to conform to standards of religious behavior, even well-intended activities?

Dennis is a deeply committed believer, and tends to think for himself; meaning that he's not satisfied with an unquestioned approach to faith. What's more, he's already strongly involved in a fellowship with people he's been walking with for years; but that fellowship isn't connected to the local church where he's playing drums.

Dennis is afraid that if he questions the mandate to participate in the worship team small group—with its scripted small group study—he'll be challenged at best, and asked to leave, at worst. His fears are not unfounded.

He knows how religious organizations conduct themselves, even well-intended ones: "Unless you follow Jesus in the way we've prescribed, your faith is suspect and your commitment is questionable." Uniformity of behavior and conformity to particular benchmarks are modus operandi of many of today's churches. Conformity makes us feel as if everyone's in agreement, pursuing the same path to righteousness: It is control masquerading as discipleship. Uniformity gives us the illusion of 'church unity,' when all it does is produce masses of cyborg Christians who have no mind of their own and are reluctant to take responsibility for their own spiritual growth.

Kept on the bottle

It becomes a rather alarming situation when religious systems keep people from thinking and acting for themselves. We have churches in America where members are being kept, even unintentionally, in their spiritual diapers with a bottle in their mouths—not knowing enough to challenge assumptions from the pulpit. For the most part, this is not their fault. Because pastors are viewed as infallible and obviously more learned and chosen than the rest of us, we can't tell when they may be mistaken. Leadership's intention is probably not be to mislead their people, but let's be frank: no one can be right all the time. Everyone has faulty assumptions and an incomplete theology. (Even this author!) Because most people in the pew have come under a false view of spiritual authority, authoritarian leaders may take advantage, even unintentionally, of their naïveté. Fear and control become operational procedures even in God's family, because divergent opinions, even Biblical ones, are not tolerated.

In his discussion on leadership in the family of God, Dallas Willard describes what we all too often witness in churches: some leaders "will invariably turn to controlling the flock through their own abilities to organize and drive, all suitably clothed in a spiritual terminology and manner." Leaders who control and drive rather than lead from humility and mutual submission forget whose Church it is. Many leaders won't tolerate the possibility they could be mistaken or that a word from the Lord might come through another in the family. They operate under the "premise that God speaks to one or several central people in the group in a way that he does not speak to the ordinary members. These members are taught not to trust their own minds or their own communications with God except within the context of the group, with all its pressures toward conformity to the word from on high." Conformity to the hive is the supreme mandate. Willard reminds us that this is the leadership behavior of cults.[27]

A wrong view of spiritual authority

I recently heard of a situation in a church that centered around the messy firing of a staff member. When the pastoral leadership met with the volunteer group that was to be most affected by the staff member's termination, one of the group members challenged the decision of the church leadership. Some of the group felt that they were being utterly left out of the decision making process and that critical choices were being made *for* them by the leadership. In response, one of the pastors said that the people must submit to the authority of the pastoral staff. The church member challenged that authoritarianism by saying, "And you [pastors] can never be wrong?" People can tell when authority is being "lorded over" them. Notice how conformity to the will of the leadership was to go unquestioned, as those adhering to law rather than operating as mutually informing members of the Body of Christ.

Notice the assumption behind the mandate to conform: church members' hearts cannot be trusted. Their will and their desires are suspect. In contrast, the will of the leadership is beyond discussion and reproach.

In contrast to this destructive and imperious leadership mentality, hear what Charles Spurgeon says: "What position is nobler than that of a spiritual father who claims no authority and yet is universally esteemed, whose word is given only as tender advice, but is allowed to operate with the force of law? Consulting the wishes of others he finds that they are glad to defer to him. Lovingly firm and graciously gentle, he is the chief of all because he is the servant of all."[28]

James' story

James was the drummer on a church's worship team. He was given strict instructions to keep the beat very simple, because as he was told, playing any heavy or complex drum fills was the 'Devil's music.' In the middle of a worship song, James decided to veer off the simple and restrained beat and played a tasteful drum fill. He was immediately kicked off the team. When James told me the story, my mouth fell open. I said, "Are you kidding me?" He was not. Notice that congregation's focus on strict adherence to an outward behavior. In fact, "godliness" was kept through a strict set of behaviors that had nothing to do with the Gospel: drum fills were not merely frowned upon out of artistic preference, they were considered 'of the Devil.' When we don't know the Gospel, we'll assume our preferences are the

Gospel itself. We'll declare as 'unholy' that which God has made no such judgment against at all. And we'll destroy our brothers and sisters in the process, not to mention our credibility in the world.

"It's not our policy."

Most churches develop extensive policies to manage people—largely because fear and control prevent leaders from trusting people. If you don't believe Jesus has given your people new hearts, your only option is to mistrust their motives. Just lay down a set of policies to keep people in line. Soon, the policy actually prevents people from relating to each other: The policy becomes the intermediary, rather than having brothers and sisters in the Body who can make decisions together as respected equals. It's one of the best ways we "lord it over" those who serve with us. Churches that live by policies prevent themselves from living relationally.

God is not a behavior-modification therapist!

It is quite possible to act like a Christian, yet live far from your heart. In fact, many sermons and teachings from the Church today amount to Christian behavior modification—getting people to *act like* Christians. The assumption is, that if you get church attenders to serve, be more committed, share their faith at work, read their Bibles and join a small group, that you've necessarily produced Christ-like transformation in them. But, in fact, this may or may not be so. It may appear that you are producing Christ-like behavior because people are involved in church programs, outreach, small group studies, and doing noble work, yet those very appearances are misleading. The external behaviors look good, yet the doer of the good deed may be living far from his new heart. We get people to act like good

Christians, yet never address the work of Jesus in the new heart. Even a godless person can act like a Christian. Churches are full of people who act like Christians, yet live far from their new hearts.

One of the flagship mega churches in America recently discovered that the strategy for spiritual growth they had been using for 30 years—into which they dumped millions of dollars and untold resources so that people could move from atheist or agonistic to mature believers—was in fact failing to produce the desired results. This church and others like it had endless programs, Bible studies, and services to accommodate the various spiritual needs of its members, had a very sizeable budget and staff, yet could not carry the spiritual seeker or new Christian into full maturity. In fact, the data reported that those who "loved God the most" were the most dissatisfied with their church experience and wanted to bail out of the organized church setting. If you were to observe this church, it would look like an active, successful church, filled with people doing good; and in many ways, that was certainly true. So why didn't the church's programs and events produce the spiritual maturity they were hoping for? Were people just busy with spiritual activities, or were they really developing into the fullness of their new life in Jesus? My fear is that this church will replace one system with another, not realizing that systems can never produce the results they hope for. Only organic, relational fellowships, living under the life of the New Covenant can produce deeply-rooted maturity.

"Spiritual" activity that ignores the heart

This mega-church's conclusion was that, "We need words that reveal the heart of each person. We want to know what moves them at the deepest levels."[29] I agree. This is the most important question the leadership can ask. Religious activity, no matter how noble, that ignores the resources of a Christian's new heart, will only produce external activity without sustaining roots in the heart—the center-most part of a person. It is no longer about conjuring up good Christian behavior. This is the very failure of the Old Covenant (old way of relating). It must be about the heart.

God is not a behavior-modification therapist. As Larry Crabb suggested in his ground-breaking book, *Connecting*, God is not interested in tinkering with our old nature in order to improve it. Nor is does he pressure us into spiritual change, or attempt to fix our old nature.[30]   Rather, as Crabb suggests, God is interested in *releasing something*—releasing a God-given goodness beneath the surface.[31] A radical purity is now the dominant force in the Christian—whether or not that goodness is always seen or acknowledged. The new heart is the headwaters from which that goodness flows. That new purity must be nurtured and affirmed in order for the "good behavior" to have roots and longevity. Only once in forty-two years have I ever heard a teaching on the new heart from a church pulpit. Without the teaching on the new heart, discipleship becomes little more than behavior management with a Christian veneer; and because it appears that we are doing and saying all the right Christian things, we assume that our ministry is fruitful when, in fact, we've simply been successful at modifying the externals. It is possible for a person to sit through sermon after sermon, lesson after lesson, year after year, doing their best to reproduce the bullet-point list of good behaviors during the following week, and never engage the deeper resources of their heart. Trying to be a good Christian will take you a certain distance; but life has a way of stripping us of pretense. Sooner or later, the person will meet a situation in which trying harder (managing appearances)—without living from the power of their new hearts—will leave them frustrated and ashamed.

Heart, first.

In fact, the way you produce the fruit of the Spirit is not by getting people to buy into certain good behaviors; you get them to mature into the *kind of transformed* person that Jesus was, to live with the heart he had, as theologian Dallas Willard suggests. The kind of heart that Jesus had is more fundamental than his good actions. Jesus' good works and noble actions were a direct outflow of an inner life lived in union with his Father and the Holy Spirit. In every moment, every decision, he lived out of a thoroughly noble and glorious heart. Behavior must flow from heart. Fruit grows and ripens only as it receives life from the vine. "Abide in me, for apart from me, you can do nothing." In other words, Jesus is indicating that "Your goodness is a direct outflow of a new reality—I am in you and you are in me—in your new heart! That's where we meet. This is the hope of your ever-increasing restoration." The internal and supernatural resources of Jesus have now become ours.

Therefore, a better approach to discipleship is to help Christians live from their new heart rather than getting them to act like good Christians. The wonderfully encouraging news is that we have the capacity to be truly good because we have been given the very heart of Jesus. We have been rescued from the futility of Christian behavior modification.

Becoming pressure-sensitive

When you're in a context in which religious pressure is the way that leadership gets people to behave better and "live uprightly," you'll likely feel a number of things: You'll believe you haven't done enough to please God or them, and you'll feel guilty about not being more committed, more serious about your faith, more giving, more something. "Should" and "ought" are the subtext of these churches. Of course, the guilty verdict isn't stated so overtly. The message is usually about your lack of commitment or sharing your faith, or something. But the foundational assumption from the pulpit or Sunday School classroom is that, "You are not doing enough" —which accumulates over time to suggest that, "*You* are not enough for God."

By contrast, when you experience a context of true Christian freedom, you'll walk away feeling more alive, more settled in your convictions about God's goodness, and *more* desiring to live for him. In this liberating setting, guilt is never needed to motivate people because people who experience God's affection won't need you to tell them they 'should' be doing this or that. They already *want* to do what God has called them to do because they are deeply aware of God's desire for them and of his glorious work in their hearts that is both already accomplished and ever-increasing in them.

CHAPTER SIX

Sabotaged spirituality

(How the gospel of religious duty

sabotages our journey)

Question: "How has religion (rather than the Gospel Jesus offered) affected your faith?"

John, from Jacksonville: "As I look back at my years as a Christian, I am sorry to say that now I see clearly that I have been actually held back in my Christian walk, because I have been receiving the message that my heart is still bad, still wicked. As a result, my expectations for the "abundant life" of which Jesus spoke, have been nil! Because of what was said on Sunday mornings, I *expected* to sin regularly! "

For years, I cringed when I heard the words, "spiritual disciplines," "quiet time," or "devotional." Honestly, I still have to fight a knee-jerk reaction to wholly dismiss anything that sounds like religious duty, in order that I might see the *spirit* behind the disciplines—reframing those practices so that I can experience more freedom and wholeness. Religion (accompanied by shame, accusation and pressure) has sabotaged the journey for many of us, taking good things God has intended for our wellness and freedom, and removed the Spirit and life from them, offering us the heaviness of religious duty instead.

A false religious duty says: "This is what good Christians do, and you better practice these things if you want to be a good Christian." And then the poor soul feels guilty for not wanting to comply, for disdaining his religious duty. Guilt and religious duty need each other.

The following is an entry from my journal:

I heard God say to me, *"You live under a lot of accusation."*

I could hear sadness and compassion in Your voice when you said this to me, Father. I know this cloud of accusation has haunted me for years: I see You as the Constant Nitpicker, perceiving You to be forever telling me I didn't do something right or well enough; or constantly over my shoulder questioning my motives and even attributing bad motives to my actions. I never feel truly pleasing to You.

… I find myself slipping into accusation when I discipline my children.

… Enough is never enough—enough praying, Bible reading, serving.

Heal me, Lord, of foul Accusation's work! I bring your Cross against it, and break agreements I've made with it, including how I've allowed accusation to damage my perceptions of Your heart for me. Holy Spirit, please heal the damage, and counsel my heart with truth.

I love you,
Jim.

Some people live under accusation and condemnation an entire lifetime, eroding their confidence in God's affection for them—placing him in the role of schoolmaster rather than rescuer, lover, and friend.

So why my strong reaction to spiritual disciplines and anything that sounded like pressure to be holy? For years I wasn't able to articulate why, but now I know: the religious spirit, or the 'gospel' of pressure and duty, has so distorted my understanding of life in Christ that I have a visceral reaction to anything that smacks of legalism or duty. I had been taught the "ought-to" gospel for so long that my heart finally said, "No! I don't want more pressure to be holy. That can't be all there is!" I suspect that my heart rejected this new legalism because it wanted *life*— not pressure to be good, not right religious externals—but life." Please know that by "life," I *do not* mean permission to do whatever we want to do. Rather, I mean a fullness, wholeness, and vitality that Jesus himself enjoyed. Isn't a full-hearted life the thing we are seeking? Isn't this the offer of Jesus?

The means for wholeness and life

I know now that there is a vital place for spiritual disciples, but my reason for engaging them is now becoming wholly different. Prayer, Scripture, solitude and the spiritual practices are no longer ends in themselves, but the path to getting more of what my heart really wants: the life, presence and exuberant strength of Jesus himself. In fact, as Dwight Edwards, author of *Revolution Within*, suggests, "true obedience is the unrestrained indulgence of our new nature."[32] We can now *really* enjoy all that is good. Before receiving our new nature, we could not.

But I confess to you that it is still a struggle. I still fight the instinctive repulsion of any valid spiritual habit; yet I'm learning to embrace those timeless disciplines in order that I might allow Jesus to come to me with his life, the life for which my heart is so desperate for these days. Ours is always a search for life. And thankfully, that's the offer of Jesus: "I have come that you might have life, and have it to the full." (John 10:10) "In him was life, and that life was the light of men." (John 1:4) "... for the letter [of the Law] kills, *but the Spirit gives life*." (2 Cor. 3:6)

But don't we typically interpret those verses on 'life' to mean "life after death," or "the life to come" rather than the life here and now? This is part of our problem. Dallas Willard suggests that a perfectly adequate understanding of 'salvation' in the New Testament is 'life.'[33] The Gospel is an offer of life, a vibrancy of heart and being, lived in the very vitality of Jesus himself—this moment. The spiritual disciplines, therefore, are the way we connect with Jesus and his overflow of life.

Equally important, we must realize that this life is no longer something outside of us, but rather an already-present wellspring within us. (Psalm 4:23) It is not something the Christian must grasp for. That life is in fact Jesus himself, or as Paul says, "Christ in you, the hope of glory." (Col. 1:27) In other words, we're not trying to get something from God that he hasn't already supplied. Further, when he meets our need, he doesn't give us a sermon, teaching audio, or pill. He gives *himself*—within us—for us. So when we ask Jesus to 'come,' he has in fact already come. In his own humility, he has bound himself to us forever. What has always been his is now ours. The same Christ who ate fish from the Sea of Galilee, spoke Hebrew and Aramaic, and whose Spirit blew through an upper room at Pentacost, now lives in another body—yours. This is our only hope, not merely for later, but in this moment.

The gospel of pressure has come against this life and offered a substitute and imposter: religious duty. It seems holy, it appears righteous, but it is a ruse. This is nothing new, for religious obligation has always been the preferred substitute for life in Jesus. Yet, legalistic rightness cannot reproduce life. Duty and pressure cannot be sustained forever: at some point the heart will cry, "No more!"

John's story

Recently, my friend, John, told me how heart-less religious duty and performance (just do the right thing), and institutionalized faith had affected his journey. This posture of religious obligation *that ignores the heart* is often called the "religious spirit." Here's what John told me in an email:

My first experience in Christian fellowship after I became a believer was in a large Bible-believing institutional church where knowledge was equated with Christian maturity. The heart was rarely mentioned at all, and when it was, it was in the context of emotion. I came to understand that if one had deep feelings about anything, that indicated they "had a heart." I was led to believe that it was rare to find men with hearts in the church. I actually had an elder in the church tell me he wished he had a heart like mine, "but," he said matter-of-factly, "I just don't."

In the subsequent 12 years or so, in the same denomination but different location, that attitude was pretty much the same. Personal interests or desires, let alone passions, were rarely discussed. The concept of "heart" was restricted to the synonym of emotion. The message from the leadership was always more about duty and responsibility. The common theme was simply that Jesus died for our sins and thus, out of gratitude, we should live lives like this...

The religious spirit facilitated an inappropriate comfort zone in my experience in the church body. It did that by justifying the laying aside of passion and the asking of difficult questions. I was confused by much of the Scripture that was quoted and how it related to my life now. It actually seemed like all that was required of me was to know what the Bible said, and then, somehow, when verses were said, we were expected to make the application to our own lives without honest questions. It was all Greek...all didactic, with very little opportunity for questions.

Because everyone was silent, we were like a bunch of cattle going through the rituals of activities, never being challenged. In retrospect, it was settling into an environment which was arrogant and boring...and lacking in life. The religious spirit promoted the attitude of "not rocking the boat" above all, and it was promoted by "strong leadership" which was really very weak...a group of men hiding from difficult questions in their rote memorization of theology. Amazing. For a very long time I allowed my own independent thought, along with my passion, to be locked up, and I actually sought to do the same thing to others.

The religious spirit caused me to put my faith in theology created by men. I had faith in faith, but not in God. I worshipped the Bible rather than its author, and the natural consequence of all that was that I was kept at a distance from the source of life; I was kept from the very intimate, "personal relationship" with Jesus which was being advocated from the pulpit.

Do you hear the themes? Duty. Responsibility. Don't ask questions. Don't rock the boat. Forget your heart and abandon your desires. And the result? —You live far from your heart and far from God's heart.

I also asked John another question: "What have you been told about your heart—even after you became a Christian?" In other words, was John hearing a message that he wasn't supposed to trust his heart, that there was largely sin and rebellion at the core of his nature? Was the underlying message from the pulpit that he was never doing enough for God and really didn't want to do God's will anyway? Or was John hearing a more positive message about his heart, *especially after becoming a believer in Jesus*? Here's what John said:

> In my 28 years as a Christian, I have never experienced a celebration of [the following] truths from Romans 8: ... Because of Jesus Christ, we as Christians *do not* live according to the sinful nature (8:4), *we do* have our minds set on what the Holy Spirit desires (8:5), and we *are not* controlled by the sinful nature (8:9)! Our hearts are now good! Sin is no longer the biggest thing which is true about us!

> As I look back at my years as a Christian, I am sorry to say that now I see clearly that I have been actually held back in my Christian walk, because I have been receiving the message that my heart is still bad, still wicked. As a result, my expectations for the "abundant life" of which Jesus spoke, have been nil! Because of what was said on Sunday mornings, I expected to sin regularly!

Did you notice in John's response that the erroneous message he was hearing from pulpits actually sabotaged the work of Christ in him?

Old Covenant Cataracts

You will read Scripture through whatever lens you've been given. For decades, I mis-read the Scriptures as a way to behave better so that I could act like a good Christian. Others I know have been mislead as well. In fact, one man I know told me, "The four Gospels are about how we behave." Is that what Jesus came for? —"I have come that you might *behave*."?

The commands of Jesus as well as Paul's strong guidance to young churches felt heavy and wearisome to me. The commands became admonitions to avoid certain behaviors and take on other ones, lest God be displeased. I was never told Jesus had given me a new and pure heart or the supernatural power for good that comes with it. I was left reading the New Covenant through an Old Covenant mentality. After a while, one begins to resent God and despise the Christian life for requiring something, without providing the power to carry it out.

From early on

"Those who look to him are radiant;
their faces are never covered with shame."
– Psalm 34:5

During my grade school and early teen years, I was tortured by guilt—for doing things that weren't wrong. I questioned my every thought, every act. Every motive was examined in forensic fashion, as if my inner life was forever under investigation. I was micromanaging my thought life and any course of action I took. There was no rational reason for the level of condemnation I was feeling. I would confess my "wrong" thoughts and acts and find only temporary relief. Let me be clear: my thoughts and actions were *not* immoral by anyone's standards, even God's.

Why was this happening to me? To be quite honest, I'm still not sure. I suspect it is a combination and accumulation of messages I heard as a child. My guess is that the Enemy's warfare against my heart began early in my life, as it does with each of us. The Enemy begins to go after us when we are young, and comes to 'steal, kill and destroy' the budding life within the child. The Devil doesn't wait until we're older and stronger and more skilled at resisting him. He watches us closely for weaknesses and vulnerabilities. The Scriptures call him the Accuser of the Brethren, and he comes alongside us to whisper, "You are an awful creature. How could you think that? No one else would ever do that. You are shameful." The Evil One layers accusation upon accusation until we finally believe that we really are that awful creature. He lies to us with foul breath, convicting us of sin and judgment, often where there is no basis for either.

I continued to drown in unreasonable guilt the older I grew, and found myself obsessively occupied with confession. My internal dialogue went like this: "Don't think that: it's wrong. You're disobeying God, now. You're moving away from him. You'd better confess or you'll be lost forever." (I'm not even a Catholic, let alone a "fallen" Catholic as my good friend calls himself. Yet I've discovered that Evangelicals are just as prone to shame and guilt as any, in large part because we're still preaching the Old Covenant way of relating to our Father.) In fact, my evangelical heritage would often seize upon the following verse as a means of managing people's sin: "If we confess our sins, he is faithful and just and will forgive us our sins and purify us from all unrighteousness." (I John 1:9) Rather than seeing this verse as a statement of Father's relentless grace, it quickly became a new legalism: "Unless you constantly confess every sin, God will not forgive you. He will remain angry and disappointed with you, and you will be lost forever."

Not a legal contract

I had forgotten that "grace covers a multitude of sins." In fact, during my years in seminary, I was so troubled by endless confessing that I sat down with a professor for whom I had great respect, and I revealed my burden to him. At the time, his advice sounded hollow and unhelpful, but upon reflection, I now understand. His response was, "You can't look at the Gospel forensically." (What are you *talking* about, sir?) What my professor meant was that to look at something forensically is to view it as a legal arrangement. I was looking at the Gospel and my relationship with God as a legal arrangement, a contract, in which one gets caught by the fine print. If anything is missed on your part, the contract is broken, and the relationship is in jeopardy.

But the Gospel isn't a new law and confession is not a new form of works-righteousness. The old equation under the Old Covenant was: "If you do "A," then God does "B." (For example, "If you confess, then God forgives.") That was the Old Covenant. The new way of relating to God is: "God has already forgiven, so receive it and live in your freedom." (Confession becomes an open channel for grace and restoration.) And, "God has already made you good, so live in your new goodness." Therefore, in the new way of relating to God, confession becomes an act of experiencing God's grace and our new purity, rather than a legalistic contract with God.

"Don't 'should' on me!"

I was much more of a Pharisee before I met my wife. Being *right* was more important than being loving. There was the usual list of behaviors-to-avoid—things "good Christians" just don't do. The ironic thing is that most of those behaviors had nothing to do with the Gospel. I was good at saying what people 'should' or 'shouldn't' be doing. Certainly, there are things that are clearly wrong and should not be done, but making the Gospel solely about "godly behavior" (a standard that changes from Pharisee to Pharisee and church to church) became my posture towards others.

As I detoxify from years lived under the Old Covenant Behavioral School, I certainly haven't stopped being concerned about the truth; however, there's a growing awareness that Jesus was full of truth *and grace*; and that truth ought to set people free rather than keep them pinned down by a religious code of behavior. Religious externalism does not lead to a deeper righteousness. Furthermore, isn't our righteousness to *exceed* the righteousness of the Pharisees? The only way for that to happen is to enjoy a goodness that proceeds from a renovated heart.

As I said, marriage has been an oh-so-helpful reminder that legalistic standards don't go over well with most people. Whenever I would offer my wife legalistic accusation, her weighted response to me would be, "Don't 'should' on me!" (It's pretty obvious what the implications of *that* metaphor are.) In other words, "Don't dump that stuff here. You're 'shoulding' on me and it stinks."

Of course we know that there are valid "shoulds" in life. God does have certain expectations of us as his children. However, when we "should" on each other, we bring to the relationship the wrong assumption about the other's heart, an assumption that God himself no longer makes: We assume the other's heart is not good, not to be trusted, and bent towards sin. This is not a biblical view of the redeemed heart. We stop entrusting their spiritual journey to God's Spirit and place ourselves in a position of spiritual superiority over the other. A little humility would go a long way.

CHAPTER SEVEN

Good and becoming good

(Becoming our new nature)

"Spiritual growth is a process of replacing temporal appearances
with eternal reality, and living out of it."
– Dan Stone & Greg Smith, *The Rest of the Gospel*[34]

"Be what you are.
This is the first step toward becoming better than you are."
– J.C. Hare & A.W. Hare

What you already have

The Scriptures talk about certain people as if they really are genuinely good, now in *this* life, not simply in heaven. For example, this is how Paul describes a fellowship of believers in Rome when he says, "I myself am convinced, my brothers, that you yourselves are *full of goodness* ..." Full of goodness—like the aroma of freshly baked bread being brought out of the oven; or the fragrance of fir tree needles when you rub them between your fingers. Full of goodness—awash with enticing purity and wholesome vitality.

When Jesus talks about goodness, he states the obvious in order to make things … more obvious: "No good tree bears bad fruit, nor does a bad tree bear good fruit." (Lk. 6:43) Jesus is stating a natural progression anyone could observe—the quality of fruit that grows on a tree is a direct result of the health or state of the tree. You can't get figs from thorn bushes or grapes from sickly briars. Those trees won't give you wholesome fruit. Just like the tree that bears fruit to its kind, he says, "The good man brings good things out of the good stored up *in his heart*, and the evil man brings evil things out of the evil stored up *in his heart*. For out of the overflow of his heart his mouth speaks." (Luke 6:45) The interior of the tree and its roots decide whether it will produce good or bad fruit. A diseased tree cannot give you the fruit you're hoping for. A good tree (heart) will. Your heart—now good—can only bear good fruit! (—Though you can still choose the old self/heart and its bad fruit.) But you don't have to.

Why would Jesus or Paul refer to some people as "good" if calling someone "good" was not an appropriate label for any person at all—even followers of Jesus? Notice how hopeful this is: it is genuinely possible for a person to become a good tree—one substantially free of disease and everything that would destroy it and its fruit: As that person receives his new heart from Jesus and learns to live from it, that goodness spreads from his heart to his whole being.

But doesn't Jesus say that "No one is good, except God alone?" Precisely: goodness belongs to God alone … *and* those he gives his goodness to. In order for us to experience the vitality, community, and strength of heart God himself enjoys, he had to give us the very thing that makes all that possible—his own good heart. All the resources of his heart are now yours.

Other places in Scripture verify the Christian's new-found purity, establishing the Christ-follower's goodness as a present reality. In Christ, we have become the "good tree:"

Already clean: "And such were some of you; but you *were* washed, but you *were* sanctified, but you *were* justified in the name of the Lord Jesus Christ, and in the Spirit of our God." (I Cor. 6:11) By this new covenant (new way of relating to God), "we *have been* made holy through the sacrifice of the body of Jesus Christ once for all." (Heb. 10:10) "…for he purified their hearts by faith." (Acts 15:9) The clean heart of Jesus is now ours.

Already alive with supernatural life: "… yet your spirit *is alive* because of righteousness." (Romans 8:10) Our spirit is no longer sick or disobedient, but alive. "In the same way, count yourselves dead to sin but *alive to God* in Christ Jesus." (Romans 6:11)

Already free from old influences: "But thanks be to God that, though you *used to be* slaves to sin …You have been set free from sin and have become slaves to *righteousness*." (Romans 6: 17, 18) "Now if I do what I do not want to do, *it is no longer I who do it*, but it is sin living in me that does it." (Romans 7:20) Notice that Paul says it is his old nature ("sin living in me") that causes him to sin. In effect, he's saying, "Sin isn't the real me!" Paul is now controlled by a different and holy nature: "[We] are controlled *not by* the sinful nature but by the Spirit …" (Romans 8:9) Paul seems to be stating this new reality as a fact. It's as if to say, "You're no longer under the authority of those old influences—no matter what it feels like to you."

Already transformed: "I have been crucified with Christ and I no longer live, but Christ lives in me." (Gal. 2:20) I used to lose heart as I read this verse: Does "I no longer live" mean there is no longer anything distinct or unique about me? Do I lose my identity when I follow Jesus? Do I have to sacrifice my individuality as part of my religious duty? Then, I began to read the verse in light of the new heart: Our *old* heart or *old* nature has been crucified and we no longer live to it. This means we get to become our true selves. Christ now lives in us: a declaration of aliveness! This isn't the annihilation of the true self—rather, it is the birth of the new and good heart, the authentic self. We don't lose our identity through our crucifixion with Jesus—rather, we gain our true and distinct identity!

Rather than trying to become a new person, we're a*lready new* : "Therefore, if anyone is in Christ, he is a new creation; the old has gone, the new has come!" (2 Cor. 5:17) When Paul says that the old self has 'gone,' he means that it has been dethroned, knocked out of center. It has been cast to the margins of our life.

In fact, our new hearts are alive with the very energy and impulses of Christ.[35] They are one in the same. There is now a unity of identity and life between the Lover and the Beloved. As Luther declared, "You are so entirely joined unto Christ, that He and you are made as it were one person; so that you may boldly say, 'I am one with Christ,' that is to say, Christ's righteousness, victory, and life are mine."[36] No, I'm not suggesting that we are gods; yet the level to which he has joined himself to us is staggering. We have not yet begun to grasp it.

Why do Christians still sin?

The true Gospel doesn't ignore sin: it simply puts it into perspective. Sin is no longer in our nature as Christians. It is possible, but not in our nature. Christians now have a propensity towards goodness and freedom. It is no longer in our nature to sin. When we sin, we're in fact choosing something irrational—a path towards burden and bondage. We sin because we have not chosen what is most alive and free in us (our new hearts). In fact, personal goodness is now something we crave because we remember that sin promises deliverance but, at best, can only provide the illusion of freedom. Goodness, by contrast, makes us free because we are living in concert with our truest selves. We choose to be yoked to our most authentic identity—alive and good persons living in the freedom Jesus himself enjoyed.

In fact, George MacDonald, who influenced C.S. Lewis more than any other writer, suggested that we sin when we give ourselves over to anything that is less than us: "A man is in bondage to whatever he cannot part with that is less than himself."[37]   Notice the gracious and noble view MacDonald holds of the redeemed person. We are of such worth to God that to give in to anything less than our own worth is sin. You don't fill new wineskins with poor wine, or healthy bodies with synthetic foods, or noble minds with depraved images. It's not what we were meant for, because those things are less than ourselves.

When we choose our new natural state, we are joining the Spirit and his work to call forth our new purity. When we live in concert with him, the old urges grow quieter, perhaps even non-existent. (Gal. 5:16)

What about Paul's struggle with sin?

There is a passage often used to justify a "bad heart" theology, even for the believer. Romans 7:15-25 is often used by well-meaning Christians to suggest that even the believer's heart is prone to sin:

> I do not understand what I do. For what I want to do I do not do, but what I hate I do… As it is, it is no longer I myself who do it, but it is sin living in me. I know that nothing good lives in me, that is, in my sinful nature. For I have the desire to do what is good, but I cannot carry it out. For what I do is not the good I want to do; no, the evil I do not want to do—this I keep on doing. Now if I do what I do not want to do, it is no longer I who do it, but it is sin living in me that does it.

> So I find this law at work: When I want to do good, evil is right there with me. For in my inner being I delight in God's law…

The above passage is an account of a good man exposing his own struggle with sin. Paul was still "in process" just as we are. There are times any of us find ourselves, like Paul, capitulating to temptation. Yet, even while struggling with sin, Paul says he still *wanted* to do what was right. An unredeemed and ruined heart would not be able to want what is right. (Romans 8:7-8) But because God has given Paul a new urge for goodness, he goes on to say, "For in my inner being, I delight in God's law." Despite his current struggle with his old nature, what he most wants is goodness and holiness. He now desires what the Spirit himself desires![38]

It's not the real me!

Paul goes even further to expose his new goodness when he indicates that though he struggles with sin, it is no longer really him: "As it is, it is no longer I myself who do it, but it is sin living in me." He separates his true self from his old self: It is his flesh (the old sinful nature) that produces the sin. "Now if I do what I do not want to do, *it is no longer I who do it*, but it is sin living in me that does it." Paul isn't making excuses for himself here; he simply says that the sinful nature (though present) is no longer who he really is. It is not his new identity (new heart) that causes him to sin, but rather, sin's relentless battle against him that produces unrighteousness. While Paul's flesh (old nature) wants to serve what is evil, in his mind (which God is also renewing), he *wants* to serve the commands of God: "So then, on the one hand I myself with my mind am serving the law of God, but on the other, with my flesh the law of sin." (Rom. 7:25)

Note: For those of you who have dug further and read the end of the passage, you may have noticed Paul seemingly indicating his *nature* was still sinful: "So then, I myself in my mind am a slave to God's law, but *in the sinful nature* a slave to the law of sin." (Romans 7:25) However, "sinful nature" can also be translated, "flesh." Of course, we still struggle with our old nature (the flesh), yet it can no longer claim the place of dominion and power it once did—that place is rightfully occupied by our new heart, alive with the Spirit of God.

What are you expecting?

On the heels of his admission of personal struggle with sin, Paul lets us know *why* sin is not his or our first nature any longer: We are *no longer* ruled by a corrupt nature but by God's goodness, because the Spirit of Christ is no longer outside of us, but within us: "You, however, are controlled *not* by the sinful nature but by the Spirit..." (Rom. 8:9) He's stating a hopeful fact. No matter the struggle with sin, you are not controlled by a bad heart. It isn't you any longer. Yes, you may still choose sin, but you must not allow your struggles with sin to define your identity: It's not in your nature any longer to be that other person. You are now under a different influence—God's own Spirit.

Most Christians believe quite the opposite—that their only choice is to give in and that they should expect to sin!

Wanted!: dead *and* alive

If our hearts have already been made good by Jesus when we trusted him, then why do we still struggle with sin? Why are we still able to blow it? In short, it's because we've not yet become accustomed to our new goodness. We're still learning to live from our good hearts. The flesh or old self, though dethroned, is still lurking at the margins of our soul; and we've been living from the false self's deceptive promises for years. Still, because we've now said 'yes' to another Lord, our hearts have been made good, but they need training. Toddlers are young and filled with great potential, but they need the savvy and affectionate guidance of their parents in order to grow into their full stature. As John Eldredge suggests, our hearts may be young and undeveloped, but now good, nonetheless.

God now wants to nourish the nascent purity he's given us. He is teaching us to live from this new heart and to interact with his Spirit in this process of training our hearts. This is the process of discipleship. Christian maturity is the process of learning to live from our new heart and choosing our new aliveness over the old self. And the choosing will not always come easily; but our hope comes when we prefer what is most alive in us and discard what is dead and barren. As we struggle through this, it will be helpful to remember that we are both dead *and* constantly dying. There is a distinct difference between crucifixion and death: We *have died* to the old self (at the same time Jesus died, once-for-all); yet we are also *still* dying to the old self. In other words, we are "crucifying the flesh" (old nature) as an on-going process. Crucifixion takes time. Death is instantaneous. Crucifixion is slower, and a painful process.[39]

Good, and also becoming good

At SturbridgeVillage, a colonial-period village in Massachusetts, crowds always gather to watch the potter at his wheel. After your eyes adjust to the candle-lit room, you find a place to watch. Peeking over the shoulder in front of you, you stand engrossed as the potter pumps the wheel with his foot and the wet earthen clump spins. It seems to give us hope to think that magnificent transformation is still possible. The earthy block of purest clay, without impurities or contaminants is all potential. It is good, but undeveloped. As we watch the wheel, we'll notice that the young lump takes shape only as it is skillfully drawn upwards by seasoned hands, defying gravity's pull. The rich, wet, clay is full of hope for what it can become; yet it won't become that until it is shaped by someone who knows what they're doing. A child's clumsy attempt at the clay won't do it, but the affectionate and skilled hands of a master artisan will.

Young. Undeveloped. Pure and rich with possibility. This is us at the instant of our re-birth: we are now good, but must allow our holy predisposition to spread, take shape, and increase. Therefore, there is a sense in which we are both already made good and also *becoming* good: "…because by one sacrifice he *has made perfect* forever those who *are being made* holy." (Heb. 10:14) Earlier in this passage in Hebrews, it says by Christ's sacrifice, we "have been made holy." And yet, we "are being made holy" in a continuing sense. How can this be?

How can it be both/and?
How can we be already good and still becoming good? We can understand this by possessing a more hopeful view of Christian transformation. Though I clearly need to increase in my new purity, I do not dismiss or forget my progress to date—I am not falling back to square one with every failure. Rather, I am always beginning with a firmly-established holiness and wholeness within me. Further, I can only change as I rest—rest in God's unshakeable favor for me. I therefore learn to live from a new purity in increasing measure while I live buoyed by his delight and already-accomplished work in me. I continue to be transformed into "ever-increasing glory." (2 Cor. 3:18) As I do this, I mature in the goodness that God has

already given me. That goodness may be as yet not *expressed*, but nevertheless still present in me. Discipleship is the process by which I enjoy and continue to express an already-present holiness and wholeness within me.

Notice another instance of how Scripture can say *both* that we are already good *and* that we are also becoming good:

"Therefore, if anyone is in Christ, he is a new creation; the old has gone, the new has come!" (2 Cor. 5:17) (Here, there's a sense of finality. Our goodness is a settled fact.)

But also ...

"Through these he has given us his very great and precious promises, so that through them you may participate in the divine nature and escape the corruption in the world caused by evil desires. For this very reason, make every effort to *add to* your faith goodness; and to goodness, knowledge; and to knowledge, self-control; and to self-control, perseverance; and to perseverance, godliness; and to godliness, brotherly kindness; and to brotherly kindness, love. For if you possess these qualities *in increasing measure*, they will keep you from being ineffective and unproductive in your knowledge of our Lord Jesus Christ. (2 Peter 1: 4-8) (Here, we have a sense of Christ's character developing in us with growing measure, over time.)

Therefore, we are good already, and increasing in that goodness as we interact with God in His now-present Kingdom.

Breeding immaturity

If the call of the Church is to transform lives, then why are churches full of some of the most relationally, emotionally, and spiritually bankrupt people around? Of course there are always exceptions. Yet, where is the consistent and widespread transformation we proclaim and long for? Where's the *restoring* work of Christ—not simply the forgiving work of Christ? Why did it take *me* over three decades to begin to find some measure of healing and restoration—though I'd been involved in the life of the Church since birth? Shouldn't churches be filled with those who are experiencing significant maturity and wholeness—a substantial healing of our minds, bodies, hearts, and an increasing ability to relate well?

I'll give a recent example: On the cul-de-sac where we live, you won't see parents out playing ball with their children or teaching them how to ride a bike. In fact, my wife and I are the only parents who play outside with our children ... and the neighbors' children. This cool December afternoon (we live in Florida, so it's not *that* cool), while the children and I were outside, one of the neighbor's little boys kept putting his shirt up over his head, laughing and enjoying himself like goofy little boys will. The boy's father came stomping out of his house, grabbed the boy roughly by the shirt and sent him inside, admonishing him sternly to put his shirt back on.

Like the other parents in the neighborhood, this dad is almost never outside playing with his boys.

As the father was going back inside, he said with a biting tone to me, "Jim, next time you see him with his shirt off, tell him to put it back on."

In that moment, I had to decide whether to let that slide or not. This was not the first instance in which this father assumed I was responsible for his son's behavior. I couldn't let this one go, especially since just two days before, his son got bloodied in a bicycle accident and I was the one who carried him home.

So, I knocked on the dad's door, and said, "Ed [not his real name], you seem pretty frustrated." Ed replied, "Well yeah … If you see my son has his shirt off, tell him to put it back on. If it was one of your kids, I'd ..." I stopped him here. I said, "Ed, here's my deal: I'm the only parent on the street who stands out here and watches over these kids. It's not my ..." And with that, Ed shut the door in my face as he rather sarcastically wished me a 'Merry Christmas.'

You should know that Ed is a Christian, very involved at a local mega-church. As far as I know, he's not a new Christian. If our churches are claiming to transform people's lives, why do we have believers who can't handle conflict, are driven by anger and other issues, and whose spiritual lives don't govern how they relate to others?   (This situation is not an isolated incident. You probably can think of similar situations.)

Perhaps the reason churches are breeding immaturity is because many are mired in teachings that focus on proper exterior behavior (service to others, participation in church activities, tithing)—while ignoring the interior resources of the believer's new heart. Like Ed, many are told to be a good servant, attend church, read their Bibles and belong to a small group, yet they end up living far from their hearts (the very center of who they are) because they are never given adequate teaching about the heart. Good things, like giving your finances to God, avoiding temptation, and reading your Bible end up not producing a growing spiritual or relational maturity, precisely because those good behaviors become divorced from the inner well-spring of the person's new heart. Our churches have lost the most critical teaching upon which all other teaching must be built: we've lost the heart.

Why haven't I heard this before?

I was finishing up a teaching session on the new heart to a group of men I had been invited to guest-teach. Ken, a long-time Christian, said with emphatic regret, "I've been in church for over a decade and have never heard this message. Why haven't I heard it before?!" It was as if Ken had been deprived of the real thing for more than a decade and had just found out he'd been cheated . Exactly.

CHAPTER EIGHT

Personal transformation –
a more hopeful view
(Transformation and the new heart)

"Discipleship is built entirely on the supernatural grace of God"

– Oswald Chambers, quoted in Dwight Edwards, *Revolution Within*[40]

"The truth is that God comes to us first to give and only afterward to receive

...He never requires anything *from* us that He hasn't already

deposited *within* us."

– Dwight Edwards, *Revolution Within*[41]

Our natural tendency?

There is a book out there in Christian bookstores about how God changes people, and it is written by two popular Christian counselors. It makes the following statement:

"We are not only responsible for our sin,

but also powerless to keep from sinning."

Nowhere in the surrounding pages did I read that this conclusion concerned only non-followers of Christ—those who have not accepted Jesus, and therefore his offer of a new heart. I have no doubt that these two good authors are well-intended in their writing and genuinely want to see lives changed. But they are wrong, quite wrong on the second half of that statement. We *are* able to keep from sinning. We are no longer powerless in the face of temptation and addiction. The Cross not only secures our forgiveness, it thoroughly alters our interior makeup. Within our new hearts, there is a new power and a new spirit that is stronger than any urge to sin— no matter how desperate things *feel* to us. (Ezekiel 36:26) We are now free to choose against sin and *for* life. We are no longer slaves to a sinful nature—because we no longer have a sinful *nature*.

What is the assumption behind the authors' statement: "… but also powerless to keep from sinning"? The discouraging conclusion one must draw is that "You, dear Christian, are forgiven and pardoned for your sorry state, but you are really no different than you've always been. You are just as likely to fall into sin as ever."

Examples of this are everywhere. Another Christian writer, whom I very much respect, says the following about herself: "I am constantly reminded of how selfish and critical my natural tendencies are." Note that she is not saying that she is *sometimes* selfish and critical, or that she sometimes chooses to live from her former nature. No, she is stating a *present natural tendency* to be selfish and critical. She is suggesting that it is still in her nature to be selfish and critical. Her self-admission sounds humble and contrite, but is founded upon wrong assumptions about her new heart.

Discipleship that engages the new heart

The above authors who write about how Christians grow suggest that the solution to our supposedly powerless condition is simply to depend more upon Jesus and his Spirit to make us holy. I want to suggest that saying we need to be more dependent upon Jesus power in us doesn't go *far enough*. It is certainly true that we must be wholly dependent upon him. However, Jesus is not an impersonal spirit inhabiting our body acting independently of us whether we want him to or not. Rather, he works in union *with* us, primarily within and through our new hearts. For God has "set his seal of ownership on us, and put his Spirit *in our hearts* as a deposit, guaranteeing what is to come." (2 Cor. 1:22) That is where the Spirit is at work—in our hearts.

This is an interactive friendship between two real persons. God respects your capacity to make decisions, function in your redeemed will, and engage his friendship as any close friend would. He's not going to transform you *without you*, bypassing your fundamental and unique personhood, mechanically imposing his will upon you. He wishes to engage you at the level of the heart rather than tinkering with your behavior.[42]

Why would he continually rescue us from particular sins or behaviors over and over again, and leave our hearts untouched? Didn't our former disease proceed *from the deep heart* (our essential nature) and progress outwards? What kind of doctor treats the symptoms and not the thing producing the symptoms?

No, Jesus is far more brilliant than this: he removes the diseased root (the old nature, our dead hearts) and replaces them with hearts that are like his own (full of the very life of Jesus and his tendencies.) He performed this spiritual surgery at our conversion to him, so that we may relate to him as fully-functioning persons.

Doesn't it make sense that as Jesus began at the level of the heart, he would continue to engage us *at the level of our new heart*? Since his solution to our former criminal nature was to give us a new heart at conversion, why would he then bypass the very solution he placed within us as we continue our journey with him? He wouldn't, because as goes our birth, so goes our growth: Just as we began our new life by receiving a new heart, we will continue the journey of maturity by engaging that very same heart. Indeed, Jesus continues to form himself in us by releasing our new holiness, by empowering the very thing he's already placed within us. His work is focused on what is now most alive in us (our new hearts), not what has already been crucified and declared dead (our flesh or old nature). He is not interested in keeping track of our sin or making it the focus of his work. He is far more interested in nourishing what is most like himself *within us*.

A presence in the room

We grow in our new goodness as we nourish ourselves on the supernatural food of the Kingdom. But that Kingdom is much closer than you think. There is no such thing as empty space. The air around you isn't void and the air in the room you occupy isn't filled with nothingness. As you glance around the room you are in, what you *don't* see is more important than what you do see—a presence is there in the room. There is a figure—waiting, without pressure—to connect with you. Further, what you also don't see is the kingdom that swept into the room with him.[43] The air around you has most truly been rarified.

Heaven enfolds you in its fragrance, energy and crackle as it whispers, "He has come for you. You're not abandoned. Look over there …"

"Heaven" is not an afterlife up in the sky, somewhere in the great beyond. Heaven is a *kingdom* that fills the space around us because God himself occupies the space around us. And, as we mature in heart, we are more aware that God is in the room. John Ortberg says, "Spiritual growth, in a sense, is simply increasing our capacity to experience the presence of God."[44]

"The most holy and necessary practice in our spiritual life is the presence of God," said Brother Lawrence.[45] As we practice his presence, we discover the settled confidence that Jesus had in his Father's ability to give him everything he needed. We also discover our Father's *desire* for us— that he rescued us and continues to rescue us in this situation or that, because he delights in us. (2 Sam. 22:20) We make his heart glad. We have been fundamentally restored and are now naturally and irrefutably *pleasing* to him.

The supernatural nourishment our reborn hearts need comes as we feast on his presence: "All human beings can now live the life of the renovated heart by nourishing ourselves constantly on his personal presence …"[46]

The Kindness of God

Pressure to be good will never change a person. God has a different approach: his *kindness* leads people to change: "…God's kindness leads you toward repentance". (Rom. 2:4) Don't we want to grow when we feel most received, most treasured? It is certainly true that kindness and niceness are not always identical. Yet, our Father will not overrun, lord-it-over, or bully us into submission. If "gentleness" and "patience" are fruit of the Spirit, then they are surely characteristic of how God moves towards us. "You catch more bees with honey than vinegar."

George MacDonald, one of the most perceptive and devoted writers of the last two-hundred years, writes of God's gracious posture towards us: "What father is not pleased with the first tottering attempt of his little one to walk? What father would be satisfied with anything but the manly step of the full-grown son?"[47] So there is clearly an expectation of appropriate growth, yet a kind-hearted graciousness for those who are "in-process." In other words, all of us.

Training the new heart is a struggle at times. We're simply not used to living from a good heart and it has yet to feel natural to us. It's much like trying to get a turtle to have the agility of a lioness. It's going to take time.

Spiritual growth is something *God* himself does in us

Growth does not come by muscling our way through it, not by spiritual pressure. —Active participation in the way of Jesus, yes; but not strong-armed striving.

Our role in transformation is to cooperate with what the Spirit is doing in us. We enter into the process by living as Jesus lived, engaging in the habits (often called "disciplines") he did. However, the weight of our dependence shifts onto God and not us, as he completes the work he began in us.[48] Our salvation didn't begin with human (natural) energy: neither can it be sustained by it. Something supernatural is required ... and has already been given to us.

But many of us have a fleeting sense of God's work in us: "Is he really here? Is he really working in me?" But God is not a fickle lover. He does not come and go from us, dropping in from time to time. His presence is not fleeting—it is relentlessly constant. He has taken a lasting beachhead in our hearts and set up camp permanently there. We are forever and unshakably bound to him: in our hearts. He has tethered himself to us, forever. Therefore, we must not think of God coming in every now and then to do some housecleaning and renovation projects. He is right now at work affectionately tending to your heart, within your heart. He is tending what he's already planted.

Spiritual growth involves action, but not striving: "The commandments can never be kept while there is a strife to keep them: the man is overwhelmed in the weight of their broken pieces. It needs a clean heart to have pure hands, all the power of a live soul to keep the law—a power of life, not of struggle; the strength of love, not the effort of duty."[49] In fact, in order to live a life where goodness comes naturally, we must depend upon the very life and vitality of God's Spirit within us—igniting the goodness he's *already* placed there. There is no other way.

Latitude

God can remain intimately and closely involved in our lives without micro-managing us. He gives us gracious latitude as part of our human dignity; and it is his desire that we use the freedom of self-will (not selfish will) and desire that maturing his sons and daughters have available to them. This freedom can be so daunting at times that we may feel we're not ready for it. In fact, there have been times when I have not wanted the level of freedom afforded me by my Father: "Will I do what is right? Can I trust his heart in this? Can I trust *my* heart in this?" Yet, the alternative is also unthinkable: a god who micromanages and nitpicks, and won't allow us to grow up into the full stature of sons and daughters.

In fact, there are times when God takes his hands off of something in order that *we* might make consequential and important choices, and thereby grow up into maturity. If a toddler's parent is always tying the child's shoes for him, he'll never learn from his own experience how to tie his own shoes and therefore remain stunted in that area. The parent is still in the room offering the gift of his presence and wisdom when appropriate, yet the child needs the experience and success of tying his own shoe. Here's what the Scottish theologian, George MacDonald, says about this:

> God does not, by the instant gift of His Spirit, make us always feel right, desire good, love purity, aspire after Him and His Will ... The truth is this: He wants to make us in His own image, *choosing* the good, *refusing* the evil. How should He effect this if He were always moving us from within, as He does at divine intervals, toward the beauty of holiness? ... For God made our individuality as well as, and a greater marvel than, our dependence; made our *apartness* from Himself, that freedom should bind us divinely dearer to Himself ... for the Godhead is still at the root, is the making root of our individuality, and the freer the man, the stronger the bond that binds him to Him who made his freedom.[50]

Notice that the gift of latitude actually leads to a *greater* intimacy with Christ. There is no fear of diminishing God's preeminence here: God is "still at the root," still the One upon whom our very breath depends; yet the freedom He affords us binds "us divinely dearer to Himself."

Furthermore, God is able to give the redeemed son or daughter gracious latitude precisely because he or she has a new and pure heart. In an effort to hear God's will on matters, God may simply say, "I trust you. You have a good heart now." Now, God is aware that we may not do what is right and good in this choice or that, yet he yearns for the connection with us that *only* free sons and daughters may share with him. He wants to guide and will speak to us often and when needed, but will not impose upon himself upon us: for the exasperated child of an overbearing parent cannot and *does not want* to draw closer. Rather, God is a lover who draws us with gracious and patient affection.

Jim's story

For over 35 years, I found the "Gospel" disappointing. It seemed to have no transforming power or genuine vitality in it, nor the ability to offer me a better Story than the one the Church had given me—"Just be a good Christian and do your duty. Go to church, read your Bible daily, do the right thing." Nor was that gospel something I found particularly worth sharing. My faith had more to do with right thinking and behavior than living in God's wild affection. Furthermore, I had not been told that the offer of God was one of personal restoration and substantial wellness; not merely an offer of forgiveness.

I think my disillusionment with the Gospel stemmed from that fact that I was given a truncated gospel. At best, I had a partial gospel that merely offered forgiveness of sins and the chance to go to Heaven. As glorious an offer as that is, it's not enough; and as I've discovered, the "get forgiven, go to Heaven" gospel is about one–third of the good news the Scriptures present to us: No one gave me the other news about the Resurrection's power to substantially restore my heart, mind and body in this life, or of the Ascension's transfer of Jesus' authority to me. The partial gospel I had in my early years was stunted, anemic and less than breathtaking. And on one major point, that "gospel" I was given was wrong: It assumed all the wrong things about a person whose heart was redeemed. It assumed their heart was still corrupt as some deep level.

So what did God do to change all that? *God gave me the rest of the Offer.* He told me his desire was to restore me, not simply forgive me. He wanted to make me well, vibrant and whole. The offer includes healing of heart, mind, soul, and body.

But something was in the way. I grew up with a whole set of religious assumptions about the heart—those damaging conclusions this book tries to expose. Like most Christians, I was told my heart was still corrupt and incapable of anything good, even though I'd trusted Christ and was supposedly a 'new creation.' How I was actually a new creation was a mystery to me. Like Lazarus, I was out of the tomb, but still tripping over tightly-bound grave clothes; and no one was there to restore me to full mobility in the Kingdom.

My freedom came after more than three decades of living as an incapacitated Christian, primarily through the writings of Larry Crabb, John Eldredge, Dwight Edwards and others who reveal the rest of Jesus' redemptive and restorative work, particularly his desire to restore the heart— at conversion. The Gospel wasn't about maintaining external standards: it was about connecting with God and others at the level of the heart. What I was reading was not a faddish or new teaching, because more recently, I'd discovered the same message of the new heart in the writings of Luther and other saints in ages past.

How could generations of people like me miss the center of the Gospel? This glaring blind spot in the evangelical circles I grew up in was certainly co-opted by the spiritual forces of evil (Ephesians 6:12) who use religious externalism to keep the Church obsessed with behavior and not the heart. This pervasive spiritual sabotage continues against the Church even today.

But more than my need to get erroneous religious assumptions off my back was my need to be delighted in. "What do you really think of me, God?" I suspect I've always been a bit afraid of what he'll say. Don't we believe that God's response would be disappointment? —"You're not doing enough to please me." Or the indictment: "I really wish you were more … (faithful, loving, obedient)." Isn't this the kind of painful assessment we think we'll hear if God lets us know what he really thinks of us? But our good Father says, "I don't want to accuse your heart: I want to heal it."

Religion (vs. the Gospel) gave me those erroneous conclusions about God's heart towards me, breeding an uneasy distance in our relationship. Rarely did I feel like I was God's *delight*, because frankly, God seemed dispassionate, remote and uninterested in the concerns of my heart. But can't God be holy, and at the same time, high-as-a-kite with joyful affection? Religion made it easy to see God as the Constant Corrector, monitoring my every act and thought with judicial reproof; yet little did I know that he was pursuing me with great and unbridled affection. I now know him as more than the rescuer of my soul—I know him as the rescuer of my *heart*. And I am more fully aware of how he *feels* about me: I am his beloved son, his constant delight. How could he not delight in what he has made good? How could he not sing over what he has fought so hard for?

The good heart and healing

Assumptions can kill. More accurately, bad assumptions can kill. Mark Twain once said that, "There are two times in a man's life when he should not speculate: when he can't afford it and when he can." Our tendency when approaching another person's needs is to make assumptions like: "Oh, I know what's going on here." Or, "I bet the reason he's struggling with this is because …" A better approach to relating is to start with humility's blank slate. Resist the urge to make snap judgments about what's going on in a person. Rather, pray: "Father, show me your heart for this person. What's going on here? What do you want to do? Let me offer what is most life-giving without trying to fix them."

Often, the pain a person is experiencing is not the result of their sin or bad choices. Rather, a good heart may be wounded. The pain of the past can reattach itself to the new heart we've received in Jesus, creating continuing distress that sabotages the very life we want. So we ask our Father to do what he's been longing to do: we ask him to heal us. No amount of *analysis* of the past will heal us. Understanding the roots of your pain is a step in the right direction, but won't take you far enough: Only healing heals. We give God permission to heal us.

The heart has its enemies

Not only is the heart sabotaged by wounds of the past and present, but it can also be pinned down by three different adversaries. The new heart has three enemies: the ruined heart (old self),[51] the ruined world (the collective ruin of a group, subculture, or nation), and the ruined angels (Satan and the angels that fell with him). How does this foul trio conspire against our new hearts?

Enemy #1: The ruined heart

The old nature (ruined and opposed to life with God) still remains within us, yet is no longer central to us. Emanating from the old heart, the ruined self was disempowered when Jesus replaced the old, corrupt heart with a new, glorious and clean one. The old heart has been dethroned and cast to the outer edges, though it may often *feel* close to the center. The ruined heart, though disarmed by the work of Christ, still lures us with its corrupt desires and motives: "You want that. Don't wait, don't trust. What you want is relief. Get it now."

However, relief and life are not always the same. Since we now have a new and glorious heart at the center of our souls, we are free to say, 'no;' that's *no longer* what I want. I want *life*.

But there is a second enemy …

Enemy #2: The ruined world

We must be present to the world without being absorbed into it; identifying with it while not being identified *by* it. We must remain wholly distinct from the world so that we may remain relevant to it. The world is the collective distrust of God's heart, and therefore all vain attempts to pursue life—while killing the soul. It is mock-life, "reality-t.v." at a soul level. It is the rule of shame and debasement; the willful refusal of our own glory.

The ruined world is brilliantly represented by the dwarves in C.S. Lewis' *The Last Battle*. When Aslan the great Lion (the Christ figure) comes at last to restore all of Narnia, the dwarves had neither eyes to see nor ears to hear. Though the sky was deep blue like a warm spring day, they could only see darkness and shadow. Though Lucy presents them with fresh-picked flowers, they are repulsed by what they believe to be the stench of trash. In an attempt to break through to the dwarves so that they may see, Aslan shakes his glorious mane and instantly, a delicious feast of pies and other delights is spread out before the dwarves Yet the dwarves, "couldn't taste it properly." What was actually delicious and good tasted like ordinary barnyard scraps of turnip or old cabbage to the dwarves. The wine tasted like dirty water to them as they spit it out on the ground.

The dwarves' dark captivity lay in their tragic inability to see what was plainly visible. They were determined not to be fooled by the truth and taken in—"so afraid of being taken in that they cannot be taken out." They refused their own rescue.

"You see," said Aslan. "They will not let us help them. They have chosen cunning instead of belief."[52]

Enemy #3: The ruined angels

In his classis book, *The Screwtape Letters*, C.S. Lewis gives us a series of correspondences between Uncle Screwtape, a seasoned and fiendish devil, and his young apprentice and nephew, Wormwood. The goal of young Wormwood's sinister training is the winning of souls for the High Command, Lucifer himself.

In the following correspondence, Uncle Screwtape answers his nephew's question as to whether or not Wormwood should keep his foul presence concealed from "the patient" (victim).

My Dear Wormwood,

I wonder you should ask me whether it is essential to keep the patient in ignorance of your own existence. That question, at least for the present phase of the struggle, has been answered for us by the High Command. Our policy, for the moment, is to conceal ourselves....

I do not think you will have much difficulty in keeping the patient in the dark. The fact that "devils" are predominantly *comic* figures in the modern imagination will help you. If any faint suspicion of your existence begins to arise in his mind, suggest to him a picture of something in red tights, and persuade him that since he cannot believe in that (it is an old textbook method of confusing them) he therefore cannot believe in you.[53]

The Accuser, one of Scripture's monikers for the Devil, trains his minions to remain hidden and undetectable for as long as possible: They are well-practiced in the art of war. In fact, as I was writing this very book, the Enemy was clever yet sadly predictable with his baneful attempts to sabotage the project. While writing the book, I began struggling more than usual with particular habits. Soon, condemnation and despair settled in as I began believing that my own heart was not as good as I thought it was, and that Christ couldn't help me. Was my own transformed life a sham? I felt I would be stuck in the bondage of my habits and the futility of trying harder for the rest of my life. I feared the Gospel I had been writing about couldn't help me. So the work of the Enemy was two-fold: "Undermine Jim's own sense of God's work in his life so that shame is all he has left; and destroy Jim's confidence in the Gospel of Jesus to work affectively in his own life. Unravel his convictions so that he can no longer believe them or write about them."

So I'm learning how to fight for and protect my heart and my precious family: At the beginning of each day and before my family goes to bed, I pray a very particular pray for us, part of which acknowledges the ongoing battle for our hearts. As part of what I pray, I bring the Cross (which Scripture says *disarms* the Enemy and his forces) against any ruined angels who would lie to me and my family about our Father's good heart *and the good hearts he has given us.*

So we live from the heart, aware and alert to all that could come against our new life. But there is another enemy of our heart—religion itself.

I am not speaking of the Gospel or the Kingdom Jesus brings among us: I speak of that false substitute that still insists that the believer's heart it dark and not to be trusted. And perhaps one of the most damaging things that religion does to its own people is to shut down the desires of their hearts.

CHAPTER NINE

Desire and the good heart

(Recovering our deepest longings)

"Love is the irresistible desire to be irresistibly desired."

– the poet, Robert Frost

"Desire is the very essence of man."

– Baruch Spinoza, Dutch philosopher

Recovering desire

Contemporary Christianity often urges us to forsake our desires and calls it "taking up the Cross." As John Eldredge says, "The Church kills desire and calls it sanctification."[54] There is the injurious assumption that in order to take up your cross you must usually deny what you most deeply want: "Just do what God (or the church) wants you to do, whether you want to or not—always and without question." Now, of course obedience is critical and God warrants our highest allegiance. Obedience does demonstrate our love for God. And, there are times when what we desire is not in God's best interest for us or others. Yet notice the assumption behind the obedience–that–rejects–desire approach: "God wants your dutiful, robotic obedience. Love is solely an obligated and compelled compliance. The deep longings of your heart are not important to him. Just obey."

Is this how God wants to be loved? Doesn't God want to be *desired*? Is this how you want to be loved? Don't you want to be desired, rather than robotically obeyed by those under your care—by your children, your friends, your employees? Rather than prodded into duty, we find that those who experience the wild affection of God don't need to be told to love or to "do the right thing."

Misunderstanding "like" and "love"

We often talk about the distinction between "like" and "love." For instance, "I'd like to move here," or "I'd like a more meaningful job," or "I'd like it if my spouse felt more strongly about this issue." We say that you can't always do the things you'd like or want to do, but you better do all the things you *should* do (i.e., the "loving" thing to do.) Love gets tied to "shoulds" and "like" gets tied to selfishness. Now, certainly, there's some truth in this. There are, of course, actions that are the loving thing to do whether or not I want to do them. I may not *like* disciplining my children, but a refusal to firmly guide them would not be the loving thing to do for them. And, to do all the things I'd like to do may not, in fact, be in my or anyone else's best interests.

However, to view "like" and "love" in constant opposition to one another creates a distortion of both. In other words, we'll soon see love as something we do only because it's the "right thing." Love devolves into a mechanical obedience devoid of desire ... and therefore of *heart*. This view pits "love" and "like" against one another, assuming that our likes (desires) will always tend to be selfish and poorly motivated. But like is not the enemy of love.

God doesn't merely tolerate us: He wants us. He *likes* us. (Remember, we are now likeable new creations.)

Wouldn't it be more consistent with our understanding of the new heart to say that through our renovated hearts, God has transformed our "likes" so that he can now give us the deep longings ("likes") of our hearts? "Delight in the Lord, and he will give you the desires of your heart." Yet, most Christians have been repeatedly told that we really don't delight in God, so how could he give us the desires of our hearts? After hearing that message over years, we'll begin to believe that we don't really love God and perhaps never will. But this is not what Scripture indicates: Equipped with a new and pure heart, your best desires are now *for* God. Those desires may be buried or long ignored, yet he is now your deepest longing. You really do have a thirst for God: "As the deer pants for streams of water, so my soul pants for you, O God." (Ps. 42:1) Because of the new desires residing in your new heart, even your "likes" can become the very means by which you bring delight to him. The very thing you most want to do can be precisely his will for life.

The desires of our heart have been sanctified. If Jesus comes to redeem, then he has come to redeem the whole person—including our desires.

Lover or statistician?

In fact, God longs more deeply than we know. Does he not desire you? God doesn't simply need you—he *wants* you. You're not merely useful to him: you are his prize. Surely God doesn't love us simply because it's the right thing for him to do.

Don't we know people who have lost vitality because they have lost desire? Don't they seem distant, unengaged—like they've lost something? Jesus was anything but disengaged. Perhaps Jesus suffered greatly because he desired greatly.

God desires because he is a lover not a statistician: He does not make decisions or move towards us based upon cold calculations and optimal outcomes. Neither should we. Isn't the *Song of Solomon* a parable of God's visceral longing for us? When I met my wife and got to know her, I married her because I *wanted* her. She was the fulfillment of those things I most deeply desired in a woman. (I was able to recognize this *only because* I was aware of what I most deeply wanted. People who don't know what they want can never find what they want.) In fact, during my dating years, friends would suggest I was being too picky, too choosy in my specific longings for a mate, but I held firmly to my desires. Later, God confirmed all this within a year or so into our marriage. With beautiful clarity, he whispered: "Here she is Jim. I honored your specific desires. In fact, *I also* wanted precisely this kind of woman for you. Here she is." Did you notice the sweet conjoining of my desires and God's desires?

Since God will not dismiss our heart's deep longings, why should we?

Discerning desire

Certainly we need to be mature in discerning where any particular desire stems from. Desire can come from our good hearts, or desires can rise up from our old nature, or be whispered to us by our Enemy. I remember the time when my wife and I were leading music at a retreat for teenagers. One of the adult leaders was "being real" with the crowd of students as she discussed her recent divorce. She justified the decision to get divorced because "God wanted her to be happy." She made no mention of infidelity in the marriage or abuses that would justify intervention, or abuses of any kind. She simply implied that her personal happiness was being violated. As I listened, I thought that perhaps God wanted her to be *whole*, and not simply happy. Isn't wholeness, joy and wellness more substantial and less fleeting than happiness?

Clearly this woman's rationale came from somewhere other than God; and it was a position she not only made public, but was legitimizing in front of a crowd of teens who looked to her for guidance. This dear woman had a good heart, yet was not living from it while she used God to justify her need to be divorced and (supposedly) happy. Was she listening to another voice—a whisper from the dark? —Her old nature? —The world? —A combination of the three? In any case, not all desires and decisions proceed from a person's good heart. We all know of people, including ourselves, who have made foolish choices from a place other than their good heart.

Yet, while keeping the need for discernment in front of us, it is sadly true that many Christians have been taught to abandon the desires of their heart.

Packhorse Christians

Many of us who have been Christians for a while believe our job is to be God's packhorse— our duty is to pull our fair share of the load and be useful to God. After all, isn't it our rightful obligation in return for all that He's done for us? The Church loves packhorse Christians because those folks are the ones who keep the ministry machinery running. They're the people you can count on. These good people will jump in to fill any need, even if it kills them: Serve on this committee, run this event, take on this project. ... And your heart? Does *it* matter amidst all this spiritual activity? Does what *you* desire ever matter? Do you even know what the deep longings of your heart are after all these years in service?

The long road of desire

The particular way in which my own heart has been wounded over of the course of years centers around the *dismissal of desire*. There's a distinct pattern to my journey in which the accompanying message of painful events has been: "What you desire doesn't matter. You will do what you're supposed to do." Yet there is a Scripture that brings me great hope:

> "May he give you the desire of your heart and make all your plans succeed."
> — (Psalm 20:4)

Notice what the assumptions in this verse are: God wants to grant you your heart's desire. (There are, of course, desires of the flesh—the old self—but we're not talking about those.) We can now ask God to fulfill our heart's desires because the passions and appetites that came with our new heart are good. And, can I say again, that God *wants* to grant the deepest longings of your heart? Why else would he lead us into such hope, and yet, not have any intention of fulfilling those longings?

Sometimes God grants our desires on a time-table to our liking, but sometimes the way God fulfills those deep longings is not the speedy path of the hare—it is more like the laborious and plodding path of the tortoise. And the reason is this: the path of the hare would lead us into unnecessary misery and would not bring us what we long for. Let me show you how this is working in my own life ... As an author, it is all too easy to assume that success occurs when a major publishing house picks you up, or when you get an endorsement from someone who could "give you good exposure." Or, there is the assumption that a "successful" author has a calendar continuously booked with speaking engagements or media interviews. There's another tempting expectation that goes like this: "If more and more people buy my books, more people will want my expertise. As I get more and more attention, it must mean I am having a greater and greater impact. More attention and exposure means greater influence for the Kingdom."

Then I noticed a similar situation in Scripture where Jesus assumes just the opposite. Jesus has just played caterer to five-thousand people at a hillside picnic where he stuns the crowd by taking a few fish sticks and rolls and feeds Woodstock. But what caught my attention this time was how Jesus handled his own publicity:

> After the people saw the miraculous sign that Jesus did, they began to say, "Surely this is the Prophet who is to come into the world." Jesus, knowing that they intended to come and make him king by force, *withdrew* again to a mountain by himself. (John 6:14-15)

If you were offered the promotion of a lifetime, or were able to get in on the inner circle of an organization, or met someone who could give you instant far-reaching exposure, how would you respond?: "Yes! I'm in. Let's jump in running!" Would we have the level of matured restraint to say, "Wow, I'm deeply grateful, but it's not yet my time."?

Jesus' reluctance to seize the opportunity is remarkable: just as the crowds press in to give him all that he is entitled to (and he *is* entitled to be their King, after all), he hides. "Knowing that they intended to come and make him king by force," Jesus restrains himself rather than plunging into all that is rightfully his. He avoids the accolades, the exposure, the opportunity for greater influence, and he withdraws from it. "But Jesus, don't you know this move would be good for you? It would advance your mission, gain you exposure and ...."

Perhaps the timing wasn't right. Perhaps other factors needed to unfold before proceeding with the next phase of his mission. Perhaps he was listening to better Counsel. And, Jesus had an uncanny confidence in his Father's ability to bring him all he needed ... at the right time. In fact, just one chapter later, Jesus' own brothers suggest he start marketing himself better in order to gain more exposure with the people: "You ought to leave here and go to Judea, so that your disciples may see the miracles you do. No one who wants to become a public speaker acts in secret. Since you are doing these things, *show yourself to the world*." (John 7:3-4) You'd think Jesus' brothers were devising the optimal campaign strategy for their brother. "Jesus, your networking skills need a little polishing. Here's what we think you ought to do."

As I reflected on Jesus' unsettling tactics for advancing his cause, I felt the merciful rescue of God ... for me. I felt God was trying to spare me from a great loss. Though my heart has endured a good deal of painful waiting—years of waiting—for the fulfillment of my calling, I knew God was rescuing me from the early collapse of all I hoped for. The truth is, God does not immediately give us all we long for because (unlike Jesus) we often don't yet have the strength of heart to enjoy those desires. It's not that our hearts are bad· it's that they are fledgling. We're still greenhorns. Too many people have received too early exactly what they wanted (and what God eventually wanted to give them) ... and it ruined them. Their hearts, though pure, were not trained to deal with the costs of their calling, and every calling has its costs. Desire has its costs. So God waits, mercifully. And in the meantime, he raises us up to the level at which we can live gloriously in all we most deeply want.[55]

Addiction and desire

Addictions are an attempt to fulfill often legitimate desires on our terms. The addiction is actually a form of compromise, for we demand relief in a manner that preempts God's commitment to give us life in abundance. Were we to believe that God really wants to honor our deepest desires (those he himself has deposited within us), we might be less demanding, and less addicted. Most of us don't really believe that God wants to "give us the desires of our hearts." Yet, John Eldredge, author of *Desire*, poses a question to us: "Do your desires have a future?" If we take God's promise to both create and fulfill our deepest desires—those that are most unique to our hearts— wouldn't we answer with a resounding "Yes! My desires do have a future!"

So how do we respond to those unholy desires of the flesh or to the whispers of the Enemy? Because we've been recreated at the level of the heart, we can now say, "That (temptation, thought, conclusion) is *not* my heart, that's not really what I most deeply desire." When I find my thoughts or actions going in a direction I don't want them to go, I can confidently say, "That's not who I am. That's not what I really want." In fact, that is the most honest thing I can say. For example, I observe an attractive woman and find my thoughts going in a dangerous direction. To think of that woman in an inappropriate way is not my true heart towards her. It's also not my true heart to betray my marriage. It's not my heart to lust. It's no longer who I am. As I recognize this, something shifts in me almost immediately and I feel stronger, more hopeful, more resistant to the old ways. Why? Because I am now choosing what is most true of me.

Just the opposite happens if I don't believe that I have a good heart: If I believe those thoughts really are the desires of my heart, then my shame increases, hopelessness increases, and I don't have a fighting chance. I've become enslaved by my false assumptions about my heart and I've already lost the battle.

When I find myself using food to bring comfort and distraction, I can now say, "Turning to food to meet this need isn't what I really want. Doing this leads to more shame, more struggle. It won't lead to the life God has for me. This is not what I want; why am I doing this?" Is it because I'm lonely and need meaningful community for my soul? Is it because I don't have a sense of compelling mission and something to fight for, something to engage me heart, mind and strength? "God, show me how to meet this need—even if imperfectly, for now—in a way that leads to life."

The desire underneath the sin

When faced with temptation, some helpful questions to ask oneself is, "What's the true and good desire *beneath* my undesirable thoughts or behaviors? What is it that I'm really looking for? What do I most want, now? What are the passions of my new heart?" And once I discover what I most truly want, I ask God, "How can I fulfill these good desires in a healthy way, in a way that brings life?" Most of our destructive behaviors are actually misguided attempts to fulfill good desires, or the indulgence of good things used beyond their intended purpose. As philosopher Kenneth Boulding said, "We must always be on the lookout for perverse dynamic processes which carry even good things to excess. It is precisely these excesses which become the most evil things… The devil, after all, is a fallen angel."

We want life, but are going about it by cancerous means. What we want is to be truly alive—even in our struggles. Our choice is to pursue that life in a way that actually leads to wholeness and goodness, to pursue it in ways God has designed for our hearts. And, God fulfills those desires in deeply personal and person-specific ways for each of us. He knows the language of our hearts, our 'native tongue,' as songwriter David Wilcox says.

Releasing our desires

It is important to keep two things in tension simultaneously: First, your heart's desires really matter to God—often more to him than to us.

Secondly, you must release those deeply held desires to him so that *they* don't become the object of your deepest devotion. Our desires will quickly become our idols if they aren't released into God's capable hands. Yet notice that though we are to release them, we are *not* to dismiss them. We are not abandoning our desires; we are simply asking God to be our first devotion, our highest desire—rather than allowing his gifts to us to take first place. After all, it is the Giver we want the most: My children want and need *me* more than the treats or delights I can give them.

If we cannot enjoy God himself, our fulfilled desires will fail to bring the rich satisfaction God intends, because we've asked the gift to become something only the Giver can be to us. When we bring false expectations to our desires (even legitimate ones) —even when God fulfill them—they will disappoint us, because they are not our Lover and Friend himself. And you *do* want God. You *do* love him. I know this is true about your good heart.

So do not lose heart friends: Our deepest desires are close to God's heart. He has given us permission to desire again.

CHAPTER TEN

The good heart and connecting with others

(How our good hearts change the way we relate.)

"My command is this: Love each other as I have loved you."

– John 15:12

"Therefore, there is now no condemnation for those who are in Christ Jesus"

– Romans 8:1

The good heart and connecting with others

There are friendships that bring restoration and healing, and there are those that bring shame and injury. A number of years ago, I left the staff of a church because of the continual roadblocks to creativity and ministry that were present. I wasn't allowed to do what I was assured I would be able to do when I accepted the position. A friend who had known me from another church and who was now in the leadership circle of this church reacted strongly against my decision to leave his church. He said to me, "This is what you always do," —meaning, "Leaving ministry positions is something you've done a number of times before. There's something wrong with *you*." He had now defined me in terms of a perceived character flaw. In fact, it wasn't the first time he had used shame and accusation in our friendship.

What's more, he interpreted this chain of soured ministry experiences I'd had as sinful failures on my part, rather than God's hand in my life or simply the wrong context for my life and mission.

Often God uses painful job experiences to show us what he has *not* called us to. In fact, my years serving on church staffs proved to be God's catalyst for revealing my true mission.

My friend is a good man, yet a man who has easily accepted institutional expressions of Christianity, never questioning the validity of those systemic shortcomings and what the system does to good people. What often gets blamed on people is really a result of religious structures and assumptions that prevent the family of God from living as he intended. It's a "systems" failure.

Shame-based relationships

How many good people in ministry have been forced out of a congregation and shamed in the process, crushing their families and dirtying their reputations?

How many spouses learn to live with the harsh words and characterizations from their husband or wife? —"You always do that!" Or, "You never …" Or, "I wish you were more …"

How many children suspect that they are not safe and well-loved when their parents control them with accusation? —"What is wrong with you!?" Or, "Bad girl! How many times do I have to tell you?" (Why do we call a child "bad" or "good" purely based on his behavior? By connecting his goodness solely with his behavior, doesn't the child come to believe that his heart is only good when he's not disappointing us?)

Shame sabotages relationships because it makes false claims about our hearts. The assumption of shame is that your heart is not truly good, or you wouldn't have done that or thought that. Shame is based upon something that is no longer true of your heart. But it *feels true*, and that is what makes it so powerful. If our friends, spouses, and leaders don't treat us as if we have new and good hearts, then shame and accusation are likely to undermine our best efforts in relationships.

By contrast, as those who have been deeply altered towards goodness, we can now say, "That's not my true heart for this person. I don't really want to respond in this way towards them." Or, "That's not *their* true heart. Yes, their action may bring me great pain, but I know their heart is good. I am committed to their new goodness and helping them live from their deep heart. (I won't pressure them into goodness, but will relate to them as a new person.)"

The danger of assumptions

Assumptions can kill a group. A fellowship my wife and I had been leading was getting along well for over a year. We enjoyed one another's company and the group seemed to love the direction in which we were going, and there appeared to be a genuine hunger for something deeper than pop Christianity. After more than a year of growing friendships, the whole thing tanked within a two-week period. There were no warning signs or indicators something was wrong. No one in the group expressed concerns about the group's direction or my leadership; in fact, my wife and I had recently received emails from group members stating how much they valued the group and our influence in their lives. Though the reasons are perhaps more complex then I'm stating, I am convinced that wrong assumptions about the heart killed the group.

Rather than having honest conversations about the direction of the group, alliances were formed, conclusions were drawn about my motives and intentions, and the group died—with hard feelings and awkward glances lasting for months. Perhaps there was the veneer of relationship without the depth of honest community needed to push through rough waters. Maybe I could have done something differently. Maybe not. I did all I knew how to repair the situation. In any case the outcome was sad …and perhaps could have been prevented … if we trusted one another's good hearts.

The devil hates strong friendships, especially those that are rooted in the Kingdom of Jesus.

A couple years ago, I was almost taken out by a beloved friend. By that, I mean that the conversation we were engaged in was so painful for me that it nearly led to a total loss of heart. It was all I could do not to get up and walk out of the restaurant, dump the friendship and shut off all access to my heart—even to God.

My friend seemed to be making some painful assumptions about my walk with God, assuming I wasn't really yielding to God's will for my life. How I was *interpreting* my friend's words also played into our conversation. What my good friend didn't realize (and I didn't realize at the time), was that our conversation was a set-up.

While driving to the restaurant where I was to meet my friend, I had sensed the need to pray again about our upcoming time together. I had no idea why; and though I always pray for God's protection over conversations, I sensed an additional urgency to bring the Kingdom of Jesus over our time together—before I got there. I prayed briefly for the work of Jesus to cover our time together, and quite honestly, didn't give it much more thought.

I realized later why that protection would be so critical. The Enemy had intentions for that conversation. He will break up alliances within God's Kingdom whenever he gets the opportunity, and he was waiting in ambush as we sat down to enjoy one another's company. The Devil will co-opt a friend's words and will breathe a deceitful stench into each phrase; and he does so with tailor-made precision, for he knows exactly what it would take for me to lose heart.

The Enemy is not omniscient, but he is terribly cunning, and will manipulate your wounds and fears. He's been doing this for years, right under your nose.

Though my friend's painful assumptions about me were spoken in part because of some struggles in how his own journey was unfolding, he didn't realize that the devil was in the details of that conversation. Nor did I, at the time. The day after our conversation, I realized we were being manipulated by a foul presence in the room; yet though I had a better understanding of the underlying dynamics I still felt blooded and needed to go to God for some healing. My friend's heart was good and his intents towards me noble. To draw any other conclusion about his heart would deny the work of Jesus, and make fear the governing reality of our friendship. Still, though clearly not intentional, his assumptions became well-placed wounds and the bleeding didn't suddenly stop simply because I realized there was warfare set against me.

In the days following that conversation, I had to fight the temptation to draw some very dangerous conclusions of my own. Here are some cliffs I was heading towards: "This is not a safe friendship. Leave now before this happens again. In fact, no friendship will ever be safe. Don't give your heart to them."

Some of what I was hearing was what the Enemy *wanted me to hear*. If the Devil can get you to buy into one lie, he'll continue opening that door until it's off its hinges and you've lost all sense of reality. Thank God, I chose not to buy into the deception, and my friend and I continue to enjoy a wonderful friendship.

Not the first time

This isn't the first time this has happened in my friendships. There's a pattern emerging in my close male friendships: I get close to another man whom I respect and with whom I enjoy a spiritual kinship, and everything falls apart. (In this case, thankfully, it didn't. I think I'm getting wiser and stronger.) The "Accuser of the Brethren" will tailor his attack differently for each person. In my case, because relationship and community have always been especially important to me, the Devil reads those friendships, sees them deepening, and goes after them with the intent on destroying the very thing that's most important to me. After all, those deep friendships are Kingdom-alliances that threaten the Enemy, for he knows the potential they hold. His attack will often be against the things that matter most to you. In fact, the particular conclusions I was about to draw from that painful conversation would have led me to turn away from what my heart needs most—deep connection. It would have shut me down for years.

Nothing between the lines

Just today, I realized how quickly I can form all the wrong conclusions about a friend's motives. We are starting work on a new project and already, I am assuming he wants to control the process, to conform everyone else to his agenda. I'm feeling overrun and dismissed. Making matters worse, I haven't actually *talked* to him to find out what he is really thinking, but have tried to handle my frustrations through email. Everyone knows email is not the best way to work out a problem—there's no body language, no tone of voice; and emails are subject to gross misinterpretations. It's common knowledge that less than ten percent of communication is the *words* themselves. It's like writing a letter, but cutting out 90 percent of it with scissors, then sending only ten percent of the letter—and hoping that the other person understands what you're trying to say. I should have known better.

Today, after I actually spoke to my friend by phone, I discovered that none of my suspicions were true about him! I was reading between the lines, or more accurately, creating a subtext that wasn't even there. I misjudged my friend's heart because of the assumptions I was quick to form.

The Enemy loves assumptions. But now, our good hearts are our best defense against his foul play.

The new heart and family relationships

We can now parent our children from a wholly new perspective: If they know Jesus, then their hearts are now good. We now offer them discipline without accusation; consequences without condemnation. Whenever discipline is necessary, I am careful to follow up the discipline by saying to my child, "Honey, I believe your heart is good," so that they don't interpret discipline as condemnation. There is no shame any longer—only loving correction. Or, if my children are choosing their old nature by being disrespectful or unkind, I'll ask them, "Is that really your heart?" And they'll whisper, "No." By doing this, a better foundation is being laid so that they walk in the way that leads to life. As their father, it is my privilege to cooperate with God—who is more concerned with what is most like himself in them—than he is with managing their behavior.

If you and your spouse have both said 'yes' to Jesus, you have the most hopeful kind of relationship there is—despite any harm they've done to you. If you believed that your spouse's heart was good and that their truest desires were actually *for* you—whether or not they were meeting your expectations—how would that change how you relate to each other? We don't need to pretend that they are good, nor deny their failures. Rather, we rehearse their new righteousness because they actually are a different person because of Jesus. *That's* our point of connection with them. We draw new conclusions as we relate to our spouses—regardless of how things seem to be going: "Despite her subtle accusations, I know that's not her true heart towards me." Or, "Even though the pull is to shut down and find another way to meet my needs, I won't go in that direction, because my heart is *for* him now." I know that something is alive and strong in my spouse; something noble and good is beneath the painful mess—and that is what I'm most interested in. If I am to relate well, I must relate to *that* person—the one whose heart is good and pure...and *for* me.

Recovery

As you consider the message of your good heart and this more hopeful way of relating to others, you may be asking, "What do I do if I'm in a church or fellowship where the message of the new heart is not taught, or worse, opposed?"

You may have to leave that church.

Your heart is worth caring for because you cannot live without it. You cannot relate well without your heart. You cannot love anyone, especially God, without a heart that is alive and whole. It is critical that you be given space to heal, to discover the strength and desires of your new heart, and be given permission to live from it.

Ask your God, your Counselor, what he would advise you. Sometimes, after leaving a congregation or fellowship for a period of time, a person is able to heal, to get back their strength. God then, may ask him to go back into that context to be a missionary (Isn't it a sad irony that God must to send missionaries *back into the Church*—with the Gospel!?). This missionary assignment may only be for a season. My family and I left the context we were in. But God led me back into that context for a season, yet hasn't called my wife or children back into it. In the meantime, my family and I find the fellowship we need elsewhere—through individual relationships with those who have discovered this new life of the heart. It is not a perfect situation and we're often lonely when fellowship is scarce; yet we know our hearts matter to God.

There are also situations in which God releases people to leave a church permanently, giving them permission to find life-giving fellowship in other ways. In either case, God gives them space to heal and be restored from the damage of Old Covenant, heart-less relating.

"So how do you find fellowship?"
You may not … for a while. I would be doing you a disservice to imply that choosing this path is an easy one. It is not. You may be lonely for a time. But you will always be part of the Church—for God's Body is not bound to organized expressions of the faith or to scheduled weekly meetings in holy

buildings. But there is hope: There are many who are now finding Jesus outside the walls of organized religion. Yet a word of caution here: Just because a person might be part of a more organic fellowship or house church, does not always mean that group believes the New Covenant message of the good heart. They may still be drinking old wine. Again, our Counselor, the Holy Spirit, will lead us into the truth as we make these decisions.

You can ask God to connect you with a few others who are pursuing Jesus with their new hearts. There is a growing number of Christians who are finding the rest of the Gospel this book has shared with you, and are living in its freedom. Your Father knows you need this kind of fellowship and wants this for you. Most importantly, no matter what season you're in, you will always have the dear fellowship of your Father, your Brother, and your Counselor to walk with you. This Royal Fellowship is your first family.

Do not give up. God is arranging relationships for you even now that are beautiful, strong, and alive. You will find the relationships of the heart you know you were meant for.

Visit Jim's blog and listen to his podcasts at:

www.robbinswritings.com

ENDNOTES

[1] Dallas Willard, *Renovation of the Heart*, (Colorado Springs: NavPress, 2002).

[2] Jerome Groopman, M.D., *How Doctors Think*, (New York: Houghton Mifflin Company, 2007).

[3] Finnamore and Garvin, *Treasures of the Kingdom*, Vol. 1, (Coeur d'Alene: Starlight Publishing, 2007).

[4] Dallas Willard, *Renovation of the Heart,* (Colorado Springs: NavPress, 2002).

[5] Albert Einstein, quoted in Dwight Edwards, "The Rat Within: The Need for the New Covenant," sermon notes.

[6] Dallas Willlard, *Renovation of the Heart*, (Colorado Springs: NavPress, 2002).

[7] John Ortberg, *God Is Closer Than You Think*, (Grand Rapids: Zondervan, 2005).

[8] Spiros Zodhiates, ed., *Hebrew/Greek Key Study Bible*, (Chattanooga: AMG Publishers, 1984/1990). —*Kardia* ("heart")

[9] Dallas Willard, *Renovation of the Heart,* (Colorado Springs: NavPress, 2002).

[10] C.S. Lewis, *The Chronicles of Narnia–The Last Battle*, (New York: Harper Collins, 1994).

[11] Quoted in Dwight Edwards, "The New Disposition," sermon notes

[12] Quoted in Dwight Edwards, "The New Disposition," sermon notes

[13] Quoted in Dwight Edwards, "The New Disposition," sermon notes

[14] J.I. Packer, "Regeneration."

[15] Quoted in Dwight Edwards, "The New Disposition," sermon notes

[16] Quoted in Dwight Edwards, "The New Disposition," sermon notes

[17] George MacDonald, *Unspoken Sermons*, (Whitehorn: Johannesen, 2004).

[18] Dick Staub, *The Culturally Savvy Christian*, (San Francisco: Jossey-Bass, 2007).

[19] Larry Crabb, *Connecting*, (Nashville: Word, 1997).

[20] Dallas Willard, *Renovation of the Heart*, (Colorado Springs: NavPress, 2002).

[21] Larry Crabb, *Connecting*, (Nashville: Word, 1997).

[22] Larry Crabb, *Connecting*, (Nashville: Word, 1997).

[23] Anthony Mitchell, *Associated Press*; posted: 21 June, 2005; ADDIS ABABA, Ethiopia (AP)

[24] Dallas Willard, *Hearing God*, (Downers Grove: Intervarsity Press, 1999).

[25] George MacDonald, *Unspoken Sermons*, (Whitehorn: Johannesen, 2004).

[26] Quoted in Dwight Edwards, "The New Disposition," sermon notes

[27] Dallas Willard, *Hearing God*, (Downers Grove: Intervarsity Press, 1999).

[28] David Otis Fuller, ed., *Spurgeon's Lectures to His Students*, quoted in Dallas Willard, *Hearing God*, (Downers Grove: Intervarsity Press, 1999).

[29] From the website, www.revealnow.com

[30] Larry Crabb, *Connecting*, (Nashville: Word, 1997).

[31] Larry Crabb, *Connecting*, (Nashville: Word, 1997).

[32] Dwight Edwards, *Revolution Within*, (Colorado Springs: WaterBrook Press, 2001).

[33] Dallas Willard, *The Spirit of the Disciplines*, (New York: HarperCollins, 1991).

[34] Dan Stone & Greg Smith, *The Rest of the Gospel*, (Richardson: One Press, 2000).

[35] Larry Crabb, *Connecting*, (Nashville: Word, 1997).

[36] Dwight Edwards, "Our New Identity," sermon notes.

[37] C.S. Lewis, *George MacDonald* – Anthology, (New York: HarperCollins, 2001).

[38] *Romans* 8:5

[39] Dallas Willard, *Kingdom Living*, teaching audio

[40] Oswald Chambers, *My Utmost For His Highest*, quoted in Dwight Edwards, *Revolution Within*, (Colorado Springs: WaterBrook Press, 2001).

[41] Dwight Edwards, *Revolution Within*, (Colorado Springs: WaterBrook Press, 2001).

[42] Larry Crabb, in his book, *Connecting*, suggests that God is not interested in fixing us. Rather, he wants to expose us to his true self, alluring in all his goodness.

[43] Dallas Willard's teaching on the Kingdom is exceptional and wonderfully hopeful. See his book, *The Divine Conspiracy* and additional teaching tapes at www.dwillard.org.

[44] John Ortberg, *God Is Closer Than You Think*, (Grand Rapids: Zondervan, 2005).

[45] Brother Lawrence, *The Practice of the Presence of God*, (Springdale: Whitaker House, 1982).

[46] Dallas Willard, *Renovation of the Heart*, (Colorado Springs: NavPress, 2002).

[47] C.S. Lewis, *George MacDonald*, – Anthology, (New York: HarperCollins, 2001).

[48] There are many good books on the spiritual disciplines. A good place to begin is Dallas Willard's, *Spirit of the Disciplines*.

[49] C.S.Lewis, *George MacDonald* – Anthology, (New York: HarperCollins, 2001).

[50] C.S.Lewis, *George MacDonald* – Anthology, (New York: HarperCollins, 2001).

[51] Dallas Willard, *Renovation of the Heart*, (Colorado Springs: NavPress, 2002). Here, Willard discusses the state of the ruined soul.

[52] C.S. Lewis, *The Chronicles of Narnia–The Last Battle*, (New York: Harper Collins, 1994).

[53] C.S. Lewis, *The Screwtape Letters*, (Ulrichsville: Barbour Publishing, 1985).

[54] John Eldredge

[55] Gary Barkalow has a great teaching series on calling and our desires, called, *Breakthrough to Your Purpose*. It is not the usual formulaic approach to calling. www.ransomedheart.com.

Lightning Source UK Ltd.
Milton Keynes UK
UKOW051837050312

188388UK00003B/85/P